Official Guide to the

Wales Coast Path: **Llŷn Peninsula**

Bangor to Porthmadog

Porth Dinllaen, near Nefyn, on the Llŷn Peninsula

www.walescoastpath.gov.uk | www.walescoastpath.co.uk

Official Guide to the

Wales Coast Path
Llŷn Peninsula

Bangor to Porthmadog

*110 miles/ 180 kilometres of
superb coastal walking*

Carl Rogers &
Tony Bowerman

Northern Eye
Books

www.northerneyebooks.co.uk

Text: Carl Rogers and Tony Bowerman

Series editor: Tony Bowerman

Introductory section: Tony Bowerman

Photographs: © Crown copyright (2014) Visit Wales, Shutterstock, Dreamstime, Carl Rogers, Tony Bowerman, Steve Young

Design: Carl Rogers

Northern Eye Books
ISBN 978-1-908632-24-1

A CIP catalogue record for this book is available from the British Library

www.northerneyebooks.co.uk
www.top10walks.co.uk

Important Advice: The route described in this book is undertaken at the reader's own risk. Walkers should take into account their level of fitness, wear suitable footwear and clothing, and carry food and water. It is also advisable to take the relevant OS maps with you in case you get lost and leave the area covered by our maps.

Whilst every care has been taken to ensure the accuracy of the route directions, the publishers cannot accept responsibility for errors or omissions, or for changes in the details given. Nor can the publisher and copyright owners accept responsibility for any consequences arising from the use of this book.

If you find any inaccuracies in either the text or maps, please write or email us at the addresses below. Thank you.

Acknowledgements: Warm thanks are due to everyone who helped make this book a reality. Thank you, in particular, to Natural Resources Wales' who have worked on on the Wales Coast Path since 2007. Both have been generous with their friendly advice and support. Thanks, too, to the Wales Coast Path officers for each local authority along the path, tourism officers, museum and library staff, Wales on View picture researchers, freelance photographers, and everyone else who has played a part.

First published in 2014 by

Northern Eye Books Limited
Tattenhall, Cheshire CH3 9PX

Second edition published 2016

Email: tony@northerneyebooks.com

For trade and sales enquiries, please call
01928 723 744

Contents

Official Guides to the Wales Coast Path

The Official Guides to the Wales Coast Path are the only ones endorsed by **Natural Resources Wales**, the body responsible for co-ordinating the development of the route. The Official Guides split the Path into seven main sections with a guide for each. Together, they cover the entire 870-mile Path from the outskirts of Chester in the north to Chepstow in the south.

For details of the full range of Official Guides to the Wales Coast Path, see:

www.walescoastpath.gov.uk/plan-your-trip/guidebooks

Wales Coast Path
Discover the shape of a nation

WALES IS THE LARGEST COUNTRY IN THE WORLD with a continuous path around its entire coast. The **Wales Coast Path** promises 870 miles/1400 kilometres of unbroken coastal walking, from the outskirts of Chester in the north to Chepstow in the south. Along the way you'll experience the very best of Wales: stunning scenery, stirring history, Welsh culture, and wildlife in abundance. If you tackle only one big walk in your life, make it this one. It's unmissable.

Great Orme, North Wales

South Stack Lighthouse, Anglesey

Puffin with sand eels

Caernarfon Castle

Shell Island, Gwynedd

'Green Bridge of Wales', Pembrokeshire

Tenby, Pembrokeshire

Bottlenose dolphins

Three Cliffs Bay, Gower

Millennium Centre, Cardiff

Wales Coast Path
An 870-mile coastal adventure

When the **Wales Coast Path** opened in May 2012, Wales became the largest country in the world with a continuous path around its entire coast. Walkers can now enjoy unparalleled coastal walking around the Welsh seaboard from top to bottom: from the outskirts of the ancient walled city of Chester, on the Dee Estuary in the north, to the pretty market town of Chepstow, on the Severn Estuary, in the southeast.

The official, signposted and waymarked path covers roughly 870 miles/1400 kilometres and starts and finishes close to the ends of the historic 177 mile/285 kilometre Offa's Dyke National Trail. This means keen walkers can make a complete circumnavigation of Wales; a total distance of around 1,050 miles/1,685 kilometres. Ever keen for a new challenge, a few hardy walkers had already completed the full circuit within months of the Wales Coast Path's opening.

But whether you choose to walk the whole coast path in one go, in occasional sections, or a few miles at a time, you're in for a real treat. There's something new around every corner, and you'll discover places that can only be reached on foot. Visually stunning and rich in both history and wildlife, the coast path promises ever-changing views, soaring cliffs and spacious beaches, sea caves and arches, wildflowers, seabirds, seals and dolphins, as well as castles, cromlechs, coves and coastal pubs. It's a genuinely special landscape.

Bardsey Island, or Ynys Enlli, off the tip of Llŷn

This visual and ecological richness is recognised nationally and internationally. In fact, the Wales Coast Path runs through 1 Marine Nature Reserve, 1 Geopark, 2 National Parks, 3 Areas of Outstanding Natural Beauty, 3 World Heritage Sites, 7 official and unofficial nudist beaches, 11 National Nature Reserves, 14 Heritage Coasts, 17 Special Protection Areas, 21 Special Areas of Conservation, 23 Historic Landscapes, 42 Blue Flag beaches, and 111 marine Sites of Special Scientific Interest. Large stretches of coast are also managed and protected by Wildlife Trusts, the RSPB and the National Trust.

Long-distance walkers will enjoy the unbroken path, the solitude, the coast's constantly changing moods and the back-to-nature challenge. Holiday and weekend walkers can recharge their batteries, see something new, and regain an ever more necessary sense of perspective. Families can potter, play and explore. And locals can walk the dog, jog, get fit and rediscover their home patch. Whatever your preferences, the Wales Coast Path promises something for everyone.

"The Wales Coast Path took me on an amazing, ever-changing coastal adventure. I promise, you'll never look at Wales in the same light again."

Steve Webb, early end-to-end walker, June 2012

All or Part?

So, what's the best way to walk the Wales Coast Path? The 870 mile/1400 kilometre route covers the whole of the Welsh seaboard and is the longest and probably the best of all Britain's long-distance challenges.

But of course, not everyone has the time, energy or inclination to walk it all at once. Instead, most people start with a short stretch, discover they love it, and come back for more.

Section by section

1 North Wales Coast

2 Isle of Anglesey

3 Llŷn Peninsula

4 Snowdonia & Ceredigion Coast

5 Pembrokeshire Coast Path

6 Carmarthen Bay & Gower

7 South Wales Coast

1. North Wales Coast

Chester to Bangor
80 miles/125 kilometres
7 Day Sections

Undulating coast. Vast Dee estuary, traditional seaside towns, limestone headland, and Conwy mountain

2. Isle of Anglesey

Circuit of island from Menai Bridge
125 miles/200 kilometres
12 Day Sections

Grand coastal scenery from tidal straits to bays, estuaries, dunes and cliffs. Area of Outstanding Natural Beauty

3. Llŷn Peninsula

Bangor to Porthmadog
110 miles/180 kilometres
9 Day Sections

Unspoilt peninsula with bays, coves and cliffs, tipped by Bardsey Island. Area of Outstanding Natural Beauty

4. Snowdonia & Ceredigion Coast

Porthmadog to Cardigan
140 miles/225 kilometres
12 Day Sections

Low-lying dunes and big estuaries followed by steeper, grassy sea cliffs with dramatic coves and bays

5. Pembrokeshire Coast Path

Cardigan to Amroth
186 miles/300 kilometres
14 Day Sections

Varied, beautiful, popular. The Pembrokeshire Coastal Path is a National Trail and coastal National Park

6. Carmarthen Bay & Gower

Tenby to Swansea
130 miles/208 kilometres
12 Day Sections

Long sandy beaches, tidal estuaries, dramatic rocky coast. Area of Outstanding Natural Beauty

7. South Wales Coast

Swansea to Chepstow
115 miles/185 kilometres
11 Day Sections

Traditional beach resorts, seafaring and industrial landscapes. Heritage Coast, National Nature Reserves

Limestone grandeur: *A spectacular coast road winds round the Great Orme, in North Wales*

Wales: Top to Bottom

Walking the whole 870 miles/1400 kilometres of the Wales Coast Path in one go is an increasingly popular challenge. Some people have even run all the way. By a curious coincidence, the overall distance is almost exactly the same as Britain's famous top-to-bottom route, from John o' Groats to Land's End — a very long way.

The Wales Coast Path will take you from the outskirts of Chester, down the broad Dee estuary, along the North Wales coast with its traditional seaside resorts and impressive limestone headlands at Little and Great Orme, past Conwy Castle, over Conwy Mountain and on along the wooded Menai Strait. The path then loops around the rugged, offshore Isle of Anglesey, or Ynys Môn, passes the walled town of Caernarfon and its castle before heading around the remote Llŷn Peninsula with Bardsey Island balanced at its tip. From Criccieth and Porthmadog the path pushes south past Harlech castle — kissing the western rim of the Snowdonia National Park — and on down the majestic sweep of Cardigan Bay with its beautiful, open estuaries. It then rounds Pembrokeshire — Britain's only coastal National Park — with

its sparkling bays and lofty cliffs. Striding through Carmarthenshire and crossing the wide Tywi and Tâf estuaries, the path curves around the lovely Gower Peninsula into Swansea Bay. Beyond the striking Glamorgan Heritage Coast, the path runs along the Cardiff Bay waterfront to Cardiff, the lively capital of Wales. From there, it's only a short stretch alongside the broad Severn Estuary to the pretty market town of Chepstow on the Welsh-English border and the southern end of the Wales Coast Path.

Only the fittest, most determined walkers can hope to complete the entire path in 6-7 weeks, averaging 20 or so miles a day.

At a more leisurely pace — allowing time to soak up the atmosphere and enjoy the views, and with regular pauses to watch the wildlife, swim, enjoy a quiet drink or visit some of the fascinating places along the way — you should allow around three months for the whole trip.

Remember, though, the Wales Coast Path is a challenging route with plenty of rough ground, narrow paths and ups-and-downs (an overall total ascent and descent of 95,800 feet/ 29,200 metres). There are tempting detours and places to see along the way, too. So it's perhaps best to plan slightly shorter and more realistic daily distances than you might ordinarily cover.

You should also allow extra time for the unexpected, to rest or to hole up in bad weather. As a rule of thumb, it's better to be ahead of schedule, with time to enjoy the experience, rather than always having to push ahead to reach the next overnight stop.

The Official Guidebooks in this series break the path down into seven main sections (see the map on page 10), each of which is then sub-divided into carefully-planned 'Day Sections' — usually averaging around 10-15 miles each. These typically start and finish either in, or near easy-to-reach towns, villages or settlements, many of them on bus routes, and with shops, pubs, restaurants, cafés and places to stay nearby.

No matter how long it takes, walking the whole of the Wales Coast Path is a real achievement. For most of us, it would be the walk of a lifetime.

Walking around Wales a bit at a time

Yet, understandably, most people don't want to walk the whole Path in one go. Instead, they prefer to do it bit by bit, often over several years: during annual and bank holidays, over long weekends, or as the whim takes them. Done in this leisurely fashion, the walk becomes a project to ponder, plan, and take pleasure in.

A popular way to enjoy the path is to book a short holiday close to a section of the path, and do a series of day walks along the surrounding coast, returning to your base each night.

Penmon Lighthouse and Puffin Island, off the south-east coast of Anglesey

Sign of the times: *Walkers on the Wales Coast Path above Port Eynon, on the Gower Peninsula*

Some people like to catch a train (especially along the North Wales Coast), bus or taxi to the start of their day's walk and then walk back (see the information at the start of each Day Section).

Another approach is to drive to the end of your planned section and then get a pre-booked local taxi to take you back to the start; this costs only a few pounds and lets you to walk in one direction at your own pace.

If you're planning to walk a section over several days before returning to your starting point by bus or train, call Traveline on **0870 6082608** or visit **www.traveline-cymru.org.uk** for help with timetables and itineraries.

Best time to go?

Britain's main walking season runs from Easter to the end of September. Although the Wales Coast Path is delightful throughout the year, the best walking weather tends to be in late spring as well as early and late summer.

Although the Easter holiday is busy, spring is otherwise a quiet time of year. The days are lengthening and the weather getting steadily warmer. Migrant birds and basking sharks are returning to Wales from farther south. The weather is also likely to be dry.

Early summer is ideal for walking. May and June enjoy the greatest

Tidal beauty: *Looking across the Dwryd Estuary to the Italianate village of Portmeirion, in North Wales*

number of sunshine hours per day (the average for May is 225 hours, and for June 210 hours) and the lowest rainfall of the year (average for May is 50mm, June is 51mm). You'll also have the accompaniment of a spectacular array of spring flowers and the chance to see breeding sea birds at their best.

High summer is the busiest season, particularly during the school holidays in July and August. Both the beaches and the Coast Path are likely to be packed in places. Finding somewhere to stay at short notice can be tricky, too — so it's best to book well in advance. However, the long sunny days are certainly attractive, and you can often walk in shorts and a T-shirt.

By September most visitors have returned home, and you'll have the path largely to yourself. The weather remains good and the sea is still warm enough for swimming. Sunny days often stretch into September, with the first of the winter storms arriving in late September and October. Autumn also means the coastal trees and bracken are slowly turning from green to red, orange and gold.

Winter brings shorter, colder days with less sunlight and other disadvantages: unpredictable weather, stormy seas, high winds and even gales,

along with closed cafés and accommodation. But for experienced walkers, the cooler days can bring peace and solitude and a heightened sense of adventure.

Welsh weather

Like the rest of Britain, Wales is warmed by the Gulf Stream's ocean current and enjoys a temperate climate. This is particularly true of the Llŷn Peninsula. Because Wales lies in the west of Britain, the weather is generally mild but damp. Low pressure fronts typically come in off the Irish Sea from the west and southwest, hitting the coast first and then moving inland to the east. This means rain and wet weather can occur at any time of year, so you should always take good waterproofs and spare clothes with you.

For more weather or a five-day forecast, visit **www.metoffice.com** or **www.bbc.co.uk/weather**. Several premium-rate national 'Weatherlines' give up-to-date forecasts, and the Snowdonia and Pembrokeshire National Parks websites provide local information, too.

Which direction?

The Official Guide books give directions from north to south, starting in Chester and ending in Chepstow. This means walkers will enjoy the sun on their faces for much of the way. Most luggage transfer services also run in this direction. Nonetheless, the path can be tackled in either direction. It's just easier to go with the flow.

Which section?

Choosing which part of the Wales Coast Path to walk depends in part on where you live, how long you've got, and the kind of scenery you prefer.

Sections vary considerably. Arry Beresford-Webb, the first person to run the entire Path in 2012 said, 'I was stunned by the diversity of the path. Each section felt like I was going through a different country.'

Some stretches are fairly wild, while others are more developed. Parts of the Isle of Anglesey, Llŷn Peninsula, Cardigan Bay and Pembrokeshire are often remote and away from large settlements. Other stretches, such as North Wales or the South Wales Coast around Swansea, Cardiff and Newport are busier, and often close to popular seaside towns or industry.

The terrain varies too. Much of the North Wales Coast is low-lying but punctuated with occasional headlands; as are much of Cardigan Bay, Carmarthen Bay, and parts of the Glamorgan Heritage Coast.

In contrast, the Isle of Anglesey, Llŷn Peninsula, Pembrokeshire and Gower are often rocky with high sea cliffs, dramatic headlands, offshore islands and intimate coves.

Self sufficient or supported?

The other key decision for walkers is whether to arrange everything yourself or let someone else do it for you. For many people, devising their own itinerary and working out how to travel and where to stay is part of the fun. Others prefer to let one of the specialist walking holiday companies create the itinerary, book accommodation, arrange luggage transfers, meals, and side trips. The main companies are listed at the back of the book.

Accommodation

There are plenty of places to stay within easy reach of the Wales Coast Path all around Wales. Most walkers either camp or stay in bed and breakfast accommodation; usually a mix of the two. There are plenty of hostels and bunkhouses along the way but, unfortunately, they are too unevenly spaced to provide accommodation every night.

Accommodation may be fully booked during peak holiday seasons, so it's advisable to book well ahead. Local Tourist Information Centres (TICs) will often know all the local accommodation providers, know who has vacancies, and can help with booking. For late, or emergency on the spot bookings, it's also worth contacting the TICs listed at the start of each Day Section.

Backpacking

Backpacking adds an extra dimension to the walking experience: being outdoors for days at a time, watching the sunrise and sunset, gazing at the stars overhead without artificial light getting in the way. But don't underestimate how much a heavy pack can slow you down. The secret is to travel

Shell Island, or Mochras, near Harlech, in Gwynedd, North Wales

Early bird?: *A solitary walker is silhouetted against the misty sea not long after dawn*

as light as possible; the lightest tent or bivvy bag, a lightweight sleeping bag and waterproofs, and a single change of clothes.

There are plenty of official campsites along the busier sections of the Wales Coast Path. However, many are on small farms and may not advertise. Elsewhere campsites are often few and far between, and may need searching for. During peak season some may also be full, so it's advisable to book ahead. But remember, most sites are closed during the winter (typically from November to Easter, and often longer).

Unofficial 'wild camping' is a grey area. There is no legal right in Britain to 'wild camp' anywhere, including alongside the path. Every scrap of land in Britain belongs to someone, and many landowners frown on campers. So it makes sense to ask before pitching.

Unofficially, however, overnight camping is usually tolerated, so long as you pitch a small tent unobtrusively in the evening, and pack up and leave early the next morning, without leaving a trace.

Alternatively, there are popular luggage transfer services on the more established stretches of the path. For a small fee, they will pick up your rucksack and other bags and transport them to the end of your day's walk. A list of luggage transfer companies appears at the back of the book.

Clothes, boots and backpack

For those new to long distance walking, it's worth emphasising the benefits of comfortable walking boots and suitable clothing. Walking continuously, day after day, puts extra pressures on your feet. Be prepared for changes in the weather, too. Carry waterproofs and remember that several thin layers allow you to adjust your clothing as conditions change.

Checking the weather forecast before you set off each day will help you decide what to wear. If you're in the car, it's worth taking a selection of clothing for different conditions, and deciding what to wear and carry immediately before you start.

Onshore breezes can mask the strength of the sun. To avoid sunburn, or even sunstroke, remember to slap on some sunscreen and wear a hat.

Other things to take, depending on weight, include: maps, water bottle, lightweight walking poles, basic First Aid including plasters and antiseptic cream, penknife, head torch and spare batteries, chocolate, sweets or energy bars, toilet paper, a small camera, binoculars, mobile phone, and a pen and notebook. Don't forget some spare cash too; most places accept cards but finding a Cashpoint or somewhere that offers 'Cash Back' near the path can be tricky.

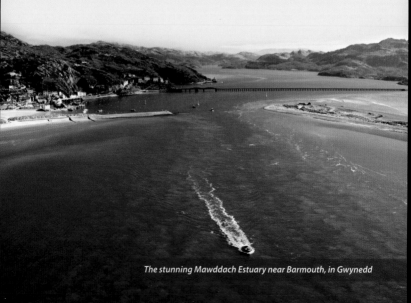

The stunning Mawddach Estuary near Barmouth, in Gwynedd

Food and Drink

Although the Official Guides try to start and end each Day Section at places with amenities, some stretches are nonetheless remote and may have few places to buy food or drink. This may be the case for several days in a row. So it makes sense to plan ahead and carry enough supplies with you.

Conversely, other stretches are well supplied with shops, pubs, cafés, restaurants and takeaways; these are indicated at the start of each Day Section.

Maps

The maps in this book are reproduced to scale from the magenta-covered Ordnance Survey Landranger 1:50,000 series, enhanced with additional information. The official route of the Wales Coast Path is highlighted in orange. The numbers on the maps correspond to those in the route description for each Day Section.

It's also worth taking the larger scale, orange-covered Ordnance Survey Explorer 1:25,000 maps with you. These show additional features such as Access Land, field boundaries, springs and wells.

Both scales of OS maps now have the official route of the Wales Coast Path marked on them as a line composed of a series of diamond symbols. Grid squares on both series of maps represent one square kilometre.

The relevant maps for each Day Section are listed at the beginning of each chapter. The grid references given in this book for the start and finish of each Day Section are from the Ordnance Survey maps.

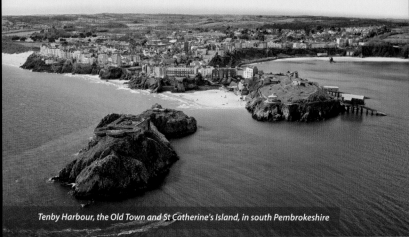

Tenby Harbour, the Old Town and St Catherine's Island, in south Pembrokeshire

Beautiful bay: *Walking on the Wales Coast Path above Three Cliffs Bay, on the Gower Peninsula*

Route finding

For the most part, the Wales Coast Path follows a single official route. In a few places, there are both official and unofficial alternative routes. Otherwise, the path hugs the coast as far is practically and legally possible, occasionally diverting inland around private estates, nature reserves, natural obstacles, estuaries, gunnery ranges and so on. The definitive route, and any occasional changes are notified on the official Wales Coast Path website.

The path uses a mixture of public rights of way: footpaths, bridleways and byways as well as lanes, open access land, beaches and some permissive paths. On most sections, the route is well-used and clear. In remote or under-used areas, however, walkers will need to pay closer attention to the maps and directions in this book.

Fingerposts and waymarkers

The Wales Coast Path is clearly signed and waymarked with its own distinctive logo: a white dragon-tailed seashell on a blue background surrounded by a yellow circlet bearing the words *'Llwybr Arfordir Cymru - Wales Coast Path'*. Look for the wood or metal fingerposts at main access points, in towns, on roadsides and lanes, and at key junctions.

Clear waymarking: *The route is clearly waymarked with plastic roundels fixed to stiles, gateposts, fences and walls*

Elsewhere, the route is clearly waymarked with plastic roundels fixed to stiles, gateposts, fences and walls. In many places the Wales Coast Path waymarkers sit alongside others for already established routes — such as the Isle of Anglesey Coastal Path or the Pembrokeshire Coast Path National Trail. In some areas these local waymarkers are still more in evidence than the official Wales Coast Path ones; and on some stretches, waymarking remains patchy.

Official route waymarkers   *Official alternative route waymarker*

Alternative routes

Two sorts of alternative route are described in the guides. The first are the **official alternative routes** that avoid remote or challenging sections; and more attractive routes that, for example, provide better views or get farther away from motor traffic.

The second are our own **unofficial alternative routes**. Many of these are beach routes below the high water mark that by their nature are not permanently available, and so do not qualify as part of the 'official route'. Others are alternative high level routes or simply 'better' or more attractive, in our opinion. Both the **official** and **unofficial alternative routes** are shown on the maps in this book as a broken orange highlight.

Detours

The directions also describe **detours** to places of interest that we think you won't want to miss. These are usually short, off the main Path, there-and-back routes, typically of no more than a kilometre or so in each direction. Suggested detours can take you to anything from a special pub, castle or church to a stunning view or waterfall. If you've got the time, they bring an extra dimension to the walk. Detours are shown on the maps as a blue broken highlight.

Temporary diversions

There may be occasional or seasonal temporary inland diversions. The reasons for them vary from land management and public safety: forestry work, cliff falls, landslips and floods, to wildlife conservation: protecting seal breeding sites, bird roosts and nesting sites, and so on. Details of the latest permanent and temporary diversions can be found on the official Wales Coast Path website under 'Route Changes'.

Tides and tide tables

As much as five percent of the Wales Coast Path runs along the foreshore, between mean high and low water. These sections are naturally affected by the tide. On the whole, the official Wales Coast Path avoids beaches and estuaries. However, beaches often provide time-honoured, direct and pleasant walking routes and are usually safely accessible, except for around 1½ hours either side of high tide. If the tide is in, or you're in any doubt, take the inland route instead.

Occasional streams and tidal creeks may also be crossed at low tide but be impassable at high water. So it is a good idea to carry tide tables with you and consult them before you set out each day. They are widely available for around £1 from coastal TICs, shops and newsagents.

Several websites also give accurate tidal predictions for locations around the UK, including downloadable five day predictions. Useful websites include: **www.bbc.co.uk/weather/coast_and_sea/tide_tables** and **www.easytide.ukho.gov.uk**.

Castle on the cliffs: *Llansteffan Castle overlooks the sands of the Tywi Estuary, in Carmarthenshire*

Safety advice

If you're new to long-distance walking, or in one of the remoter areas, please remember:

- Wear walking boots and warm, waterproof clothing.
- Take food and drink.
- Mobile signals are patchy along much of the path; let someone know where you are heading and when you expect to arrive.
- If you decide to walk along a beach, always check tide tables.
- Stay on the path and away from cliff edges.
- Take extra care in windy and/or wet conditions.
- Always supervise children and dogs.
- Follow local signs and diversions.

Emergencies

In an emergency, call 999 or 112 and ask for the service your require: Ambulance, Police, Fire or Coastguard.

Tell them your location as accurately as possible (give an OS grid reference, if possible; and look for named landmarks), how many people are in your party, and the nature of the problem.

Remember, though, that mobile signals may be poor or absent in some areas. Some coastal car parks and main beach access points have emergency telephones. Coastal pubs and shops may also have phones you can ask to use in an emergency.

Who manages the coast path?

The Wales Coast Path is co-ordinated at a national level by Natural Resources Wales and managed on the ground by the sixteen local authorities and two National Parks through which it passes.

Funding has come from the Welsh Government, the European Regional Development Fund and the local authorities themselves.

For more details, see: http://naturalresourceswales.gov.uk

The Best of Llŷn

The **Llŷn Peninsula** offers some of the finest coastal walking in North Wales. Its distinctive landscape is characterised by traditional farms, compact villages and volcanic hills encircled by the ever-present sea. Along the way, you'll pass Iron Age hillforts, pilgrims' churches, medieval castles, a hidden valley, a pub on the beach, tiny coves, sandy bays and Bardsey Island balanced at the tip of this ancient 'Land's End of Wales'. Keep an eye out, too, for seabirds, wild goats, choughs, seals, dolphins, wildflowers and butterflies. The Llŷn coast path really is a walkers' paradise.

Caernarfon Castle

Dinas Dinlle

Nant Gwrtheryn

Tŷ Coch Inn, Porth Dinllaen

Porth Iago

Bardsey Island, or Ynys Enlli

Mynydd y Graig

Hell's Mouth, or Porth Neigwl

Criccieth Castle

Black Rock Sands

Llŷn Peninsula
Part of the **Wales Coast Path**

Remote, mostly undeveloped and unspoilt, the **Llŷn Peninsula** is western Britain at its best. Sometimes called 'Snowdon's Arm', this quiet part of Wales embodies everything that makes the Wales Coast Path unique: outstanding landscapes that are rich in history and wildlife, all immersed in the timeless context of the Welsh language and culture. Lovely Llŷn is just that: a rare Celtic outland pushing 30 miles into the Irish Sea.

The Llŷn Peninsula richly deserves its 1957 designation as one of Wales' five Areas of Outstanding Natural Beauty (AONBs). In celebration of its unique character, different parts are also protected as a Heritage Coast, a European Marine Special Area of Conservation and a National Nature Reserve. There are more than 20 Sites of Special Scientific Interest, too. More than twenty miles of Llŷn's coast — roughly a quarter — are also carefully managed and protected by the National Trust.

From Bangor to Caernarfon the path runs alongside the Menai Strait and Caernarfon Bay, with the iconic, triple volcanic peaks of Yr Eifl dominating the horizon ahead. Beyond the high, heather-clad hills and the hidden valley of Nant Gwrtheryn, the northern coast between Pistyll and Mynydd Mawr is mostly empty, rocky, wild and quiet. Just off the rugged tip of the 'Land's End of Wales' lies Bardsey, or *Ynys Enlli*, the 'island of 20,000 saints'. From tiny Aberdaron the path follows the softer south coast past sandy bays, holiday honeypots: Pwllheli and Criccieth, with its crag-top castle, to popular Porthmadog at the head of Cardigan Bay.

From start to finish, it's a varied, inspiring and richly rewarding walk that should take around nine days. Please don't miss it.

"I have crawled out at last, as far as I dare, onto a bough of country that is suspended between sea and sky."

from *Retirement*, by RS Thomas: poet, Welsh activist and vicar of Aberdaron

Gorse and heather on Mynydd y Graig near Rhiw, at the western end of Llŷn

Day Section	Distance	Start	Finish
Day Section 1 Bangor to Caernarfon	12½ miles 20Km	Bangor Pier SH 585732	Caernarfon SH 477626
Day Section 2 Caernarfon to Trefor	17½ miles 28Km	Caernarfon SH 477626	Trefor Pier SH 376473
Day Section 3 Trefor to Nefyn	9¼ miles 15Km	Trefor Pier SH 376473	Nefyn (centre) SH 307405
Day Section 4 Nefyn to Porth Colmon	12 miles 19.5Km	Nefyn (church) SH 309407	Porth Colmon SH 194343
Day Section 5 Porth Colmon to Aberdaron	14 miles 22Km	Porth Colmon SH 194343	Aberdaron SH 173265
Day Section 6 Aberdaron to Hell's Mouth	11 miles 18Km	Aberdaron SH 173265	Hell's Mouth SH 284267
Day Section 7 Hell's Mouth to Llanbedrog	14 miles 22Km	Hell's Mouth SH 284267	Llanbedrog SH 330316
Day Section 8 Llanbedrog to Criccieth	15½ miles 25Km	Llanbedrog SH 330316	Criccieth SH 501379
Day Section 9 Criccieth to Porthmadog	6½ miles 10.5Km	Criccieth SH 501379	Porthmadog SH 570385

Walking the Llŷn coast

The Llŷn Peninsula section of the Wales Coast Path runs for 110 miles/ 180 kilometres between Bangor, at the northern end of the Menai Strait, to Porthmadog, at the head of Cardigan Bay.

This guide divides the path into nine logical Day Sections, each of between 6½ -17½ miles/10.5-28 kilometres. Each starts and finishes at or close to somewhere attractive and accessible, with good or reasonable facilities.

The Day Sections are shown on the chart above and map opposite.

Distance chart for key locations along the path

Miles (upper right) / *Kilometres* (lower left)

	Porthmadog	Black Rock Sands	Criccieth	Llanystumdwy	Pwllheli	Llanbedrog	Abersoch	Porth Ceiriad	Pentowyn	Rhiw	Aberdaron	Pen-y-Cil	Mynydd Mawr	Porthor	Porth Colmon	Tudweiliog	Nefyn	Trefor	Clynnog Fawr	Dinas Dinlle	Caernarfon	Felinheli	Menai Bridge	Bangor
Bangor	113	110	106	103	95	91	86	82	77	71	65	63	61	57	52	47	39	29	26	21	12	8	2	
Menai Bridge	110	107	104	101	92	88	83	80	74	68	63	61	58	54	49	45	36	27	24	18	10	5		4
Felinheli	105	102	98	95	87	83	78	74	69	63	58	55	53	49	44	40	31	21	18	13	4		9	13
Caernarfon	100	98	94	91	82	78	73	70	64	58	53	51	48	44	39	35	26	17	14	8		7	16	20
Dinas Dinlle	92	89	85	83	74	70	65	61	56	50	45	42	40	36	31	27	18	9	5		13	21	29	33
Clynnog Fawr	87	84	80	77	69	64	60	56	50	45	39	37	35	31	25	21	13	3		9	22	29	38	42
Trefor	83	81	77	74	65	61	56	53	47	41	36	34	31	27	22	18	9		5	14	27	35	43	47
Nefyn	74	71	67	65	56	52	47	43	38	32	27	25	22	18	13	9		15	21	29	42	50	58	62
Tudweiliog	65	63	59	56	47	43	38	35	29	23	18	16	13	9	4		14	29	34	43	56	64	72	76
Porth Colmon	61	58	55	52	43	39	34	30	25	19	14	12	9	5		7	21	36	41	50	63	70	79	83
Porthor	56	53	49	47	38	34	29	25	20	14	9	7	4		8	15	29	44	49	58	70	79	87	91
Mynydd Mawr	52	49	45	43	34	30	25	21	16	10	5	3		7	15	22	36	51	56	64	76	85	94	98
Pen-y-Cil	49	47	43	40	32	27	23	19	13	7	2		4	10	19	25	39	54	60	68	81	89	98	102
Aberdaron	47	44	41	38	30	25	20	17	11	5		4	7	14	23	29	43	58	63	72	85	93	101	105
Rhiw	42	39	36	33	24	20	15	11	6		8	12	16	22	31	37	51	66	72	80	93	101	110	114
Pentowyn	36	33	30	27	18	14	9	5		10	18	21	25	32	41	47	61	76	81	90	102	110	119	123
Porth Ceiriad	31	28	24	21	13	8	3		9	18	27	30	34	41	49	56	70	85	90	99	111	119	128	132
Abersoch	27	24	20	18	9	5		6	15	24	33	36	40	47	55	62	76	91	96	105	117	125	134	138
Llanbedrog	22	19	16	13	4		8	14	23	32	40	44	48	54	63	69	83	98	104	112	125	133	142	146
Pwllheli	18	15	11	9		7	14	20	29	39	47	51	55	61	69	76	90	105	110	119	132	140	149	153
Llanystumdwy	9	7	3		14	21	28	34	43	53	61	65	69	75	84	90	104	119	124	133	146	154	162	166
Criccieth	6	4		4	18	25	33	39	48	57	66	69	73	80	88	95	109	124	129	137	150	158	167	171
Black Rock Sands	3		6	10	24	31	39	45	53	63	72	75	79	86	94	101	115	130	135	143	156	164	173	177
Porthmadog		4	10	15	29	36	43	49	58	68	76	80	83	90	98	105	119	134	139	148	161	169	177	181

Distances are approximate to the nearest mile/kilometre

Kilometres

Day Sections

1: Bangor to Caernarfon

Distance: 12½ miles/ 20 kilometres

Terrain: Mainly flat, uncomplicated but varied walking alongside the Menai Strait. Sections through woodland and private estates, cycleway and waterside promenade

Points of interest: Bangor Pier, Menai Strait, Menai suspension bridge and Pont Britannia, the 'Swellies', views to Anglesey, wooded Vaynol Estate, Caernarfon Victoria dock, theatre and gallery, Caernarfon Castle and walled town

Note: Several pubs and cafés along the Menai Strait. Plenty of accommodation, toilets, post office, banks, pubs, cafés, takeaways, shops and a Tourist Information Centre at Caernarfon

2: Caernarfon to Trefor

Distance: 17½ miles/ 28 kilometres

Terrain: Quiet lanes alongside western end of Menai Strait, embankment path, seashore, and easy level lanes and roadside walking to Trefor

Points of interest: Caernarfon town, St Baglan's church in the fields, Foryd Bay nature reserve, Caernarfon Airport and Aviation Museum, Dinas Dinlle hillfort, Glynllifon Country Park, Neolithic burial chamber above Clynnog Fawr, St Beuno's Church, stone and holy well at Clynnog Fawr

Note: Indian restaurant, café and takeway in Dinas Dinlle. Garage and shop in Clynnog Fawr. Shop, post office and toilets in Trefor

3: Trefor to Nefyn

Distance: 9¼ miles/ 15 kilometres

Terrain: A strenuous climb over Yr Eifl on waymarked paths, followed by a steep descent to Nant Gwrtheyrn, and quiet field paths to Nefyn

Points of interest: Trefor village and pier, pottery, Tre'r Ceiri hillfort, jaw-dropping views, heather moorland, Nant Gwrtheyrn, disused granite quarries, Welsh National Language Centre, visitor centre and café, wild goats, St Beuno's church and holy well at Pistyll, Nefyn village and maritime museum

Note: Cafe and visitor centre in Nant Gwrtheyrn. Co-operative pub and shop at Llithfaen. Plenty of accommodation, bank, post office, pubs, cafés, takeaways and shops in Nefyn

4: Nefyn to Porth Colmon

Distance: 12 miles/ 19.5 kilometres

Terrain: Easy, gently undulating coastal and clifftop paths; occasional optional beach walking; (plus optional detour across fields to Tudweiliog village)

Points of interest: Porth Dinllaen promonotory, golf club, Iron Age promontory fort, Tŷ Coch Inn on the beach, lifeboat station, seal haul-out, coastguard lookout, Towyn beach, Porth Ysgaden, Penllech beach, tiny Porth Colmon harbour

Note: Toilets, post office, camp sites and pub in Tudweiliog. No amenities in Porth Colmon but campsites and seasonal shop inland at Llangwnnadl

5: Porth Colmon to Aberdaron

Distance: 14 miles/ 22 kilometres

Terrain: Increasingly undulating coastal and clifftop paths; rugged coastline and lowland heath; ascents and descents on Mynydd Anelog and Mynydd Mawr

Points of interest: Ruins of St Merin's church, tiny Porth Iago, 'Whistling Sands' beach at Porthor, Mynydd Carreg viewpoint, Mynydd Anelog, hut

Following the coast path near Porth Colmon

Wild coastline: *Dramatic coastal scenery near Mynydd Anelog on Day Section 5*

circles, Mynydd Mawr, coastal heathland, choughs, old coastguard station, views to Bardsey Island, ruins of St Mary's church, St Mary's Well, Pen y Cil headland, Porth Meudwy: embarkation point for Bardsey Island

Note: Seasonal beach café at Porthor/'Whistling Sands', National Trust Visitor Centre and accommodation, pubs, cafés, fish and chips, bakery, post office, and shops in Aberdaron

6: Aberdaron to Hell's Mouth

Distance: 11 miles/ 18 kilometres

Terrain: Streamside valley and quiet lanes to Porth Ysgo; field paths; elevated grassy tracks with stunning sea views; quiet road and field paths, or alternative beach walk to far end of Hell's Mouth

Points of interest: Aberdaron village, National Trust Visitor Centre, St Hywyn's church, Y Gegin Fawr pilgrim's kitchen, Porth Ysgo, Mynydd Penarfynydd, choughs, peregrines and ravens, Mynydd y Graig coastal heathland, brown hares, hut circles and sea views, Neolithic burials chambers and axe factory on Mynydd Rhiw, Plas yn Rhiw National Trust manor house, Porth Neigwl or 'Hell's Mouth' four-mile beach

Coastal hills: *Enjoying the grand views from Mynydd Penarfynydd on Day Section 6*

Note: Few amenities en route. Snacks, drinks and ice creams at National Trust shop at Plas yn Rhiw. Seasonal snack van at main Hell's Mouth car park. Pub with food at Llanengan

7: Hell's Mouth to Llanbedrog

Distance: 14 miles/ 22 kilometres

Terrain: Short beach walk; steep ascent to Mynydd Cilan; heathland and grassy clifftop path; easy descent to Abersoch; beach and dunes followed by short climb over Mynydd Tir-y-cwmwd and steep descent to Llanbedrog

Points of interest: Llanengan church, Mynydd Cilan heath and commonland, dolphin watchpoint, Porth Ceiriad beach, Abersoch 'surf village', marina and harbour, the Warren, 'Tin Man' sculpture above Llanbedrog, Plas Glyn-y-weddw art gallery, outdoor theatre and café

Note: Plenty of accommodation, bank, post office, pubs, restaurants, cafés, takeaways, shops in Abersoch. Campsite and B&Bs, pubs, cafés and shop in Llanbedrog

8: Llanbedrog to Criccieth

Distance: 15½ miles/ 25 kilometres

Terrain: Easy, mainly flat beachside walking to Pwllheli; pavements and promenade through town; short section of road and field walking around the Dwyfor Estuary; optional detour to Lloyd-George Museum at Llanystumdwy

Points of interest: St Peter's church, colourful beach huts, Carreg y Defaid point, Lôn Cob Bach nature reserve, market and harbour in Pwllheli; Lloyd-George Museum in Llanystumdwy; Dwyfor estuary; Criccieth town and Castle

Note: Plenty of accommodation, banks, post offices, pubs, cafés, shops and takeaways in both Pwllheli and Criccieth

9: Criccieth to Porthmadog

Distance: 6½ miles/ 10.5 kilometres

Terrain: Flat, easy shoreside walking around Tremadog Bay and Traeth Bach

Points of interest: Vast Black Rock Sands, Ynys Cyngar, Glaslyn Estuary, Porthmadog harbour, marina, town, Welsh Highland Railway and Ffestiniog Railway

Note: Plenty of accommodation, bank, post office, pubs, cafés, shops and Tourist Information Centre in Porthmadog

Beautiful coves along the Glaslyn Estuary near Borth-y-gest

Limited for time? — Llŷn in a nutshell

If you have limited time to explore this section of the Wales Coast Path — perhaps a weekend, or even just a day, then these key parts of the path are unmissable.

For a superb one day walk, the section between Porthor/'Whistling Sands' and Aberdaron is about as good as it gets. From a base at Aberdaron, take quiet lanes north across the peninsula to join the coast path either at Porthor (point 6 in Day Section 5), or Mynydd Anelog (joining at point 8) for a slightly shorter round, and return to Aberdaron along the coast path.

Alternatively, for a superb two-day walk, the section between Trefor and Porth Colmon is recommended. This will give you stunning views, the option to include the summit of Yr Eifl, spectacular Tre'r Ceiri hillfort, and a descent into the hidden valley of Nant Gwrtheyrn on Day One, with easier walking on the finest part of Llŷn's rugged northern coast on Day Two.

Best day walk
Around the superb, atmospheric 'Land's End' of Wales

Porthor/'Whistling Sands' to Aberdaron: 9 miles/ 14 kilometres

Use Aberdaron as a base and take lanes north to join the coast path at either point 6 or 8 in **Day Section 5**. There's a large National Trust pay and display car park with 24 hour access, visitor centre and toilets in the centre of Aberdaron; and a smaller National Trust ticketed car park at Porthor (Whistling Sands).

Bardsey Island, or Ynys Enlli

Best weekend walk
Over Yr Eifl to 'Britain's favourite beach pub'

Trefor to Porth Colmon: 26 miles/ 42 kilometres

Day One: From the harbour at Trefor — **Day Section 3** — over Yr Eifl and down past Pistyll, to finish in the centre of Nefyn.

Day Two: Day Section 4: From Nefyn to the Tŷ Coch Inn at Porth Dinllaen, and on along the low rocky coast to Porth Colmon (small free car park).

Free car park, summer toilets and emergency phone by the harbour at Trefor.

Tŷ Coch Inn, Porth Dinllaen

A brief history of Llŷn

Llŷn is rich in ancient monuments and other reminders of the distant past

Well-placed, mild and accessible, the **Llŷn Peninsula** has attracted travellers and settlers since prehistoric times. In the distant past, when much of inland Britain was an impassable morass of woodland, scrub and swamp, the only long distance routes were the ancient ridgeways hugging higher, drier ground. Goods such as stone axes, gold, amber and salt were traded over huge distances. In Wales, getting around was even more of a challenge. Mountains, forests and marshes made long distance land travel on foot or pony virtually impossible, and for thousands of years, most people journeyed by sea instead. Traders and settlers arrived along the coast from continental Europe, or from across the Irish Sea. As a result, Llŷn and Anglesey were settled long before much of inland Britain, and today prehistoric monuments: megalithic burial chambers, hut circles, standing stones, cairns and hillforts are an essential part of North Wales' rich coastal landscapes.

Standing stones and hillforts

Neolithic burial chambers originally formed the heart of early farming communities, rather like modern parish churches. When they were new, a cairn of rocks and earth covered the huge, balanced stones. Burial chambers close to the Wales Coast Path on Llŷn can be seen at: Clynnog Fawr, Tudweiliog, Rhiw, Mynydd Cilan and Llanbedrog. There is also a nationally important stone axe factory on the slopes of Mynydd Rhiw. Polished axes from here were traded for huge distances across Britain.

Society changed with the arrival of bronze tools and weapons around 2,000 BC. The climate was warm and life was settled. Bronze Age people cremated their dead and buried their remains in pottery urns beneath round earthen mounds, or 'barrows'. They also erected the enigmatic standing stones found across Wales. Look out for those along this section of the Wales Coast Path near Dinas Dinlle, Bodeilas, Llangwnnadl and Rhiw.

The stunning panorama from Tre'r Ceiri hillfort, on the summit of Yr Eifl

Coastal guardian: *Prehistoric Dinas Dinlle hillfort overlooks the beach near Caernarfon*

But as the climate became colder and wetter, around 800-500 BC, society took a turn for the worse. With the discovery of how to smelt and forge iron came cheap tools and weapons and a growing culture of violence. Communities coalesced into larger tribal groups and defended hilltop settlements developed. The largest of the so-called hillforts on Llŷn dominates the summit of one of the peaks of Yr Eifl, only a short detour from the path. Called Tre'r Ceiri, its massive drystone walls still rise to over 8 feet high and enclose the foundations of more than 150 round huts. Other Iron Age defended settlements on this section include Dinas Dinlle, Garn Boduan, Garn Fadryn, and the promontory fort at Trwyn Porth Dinllaen.

Romans and missionaries

The Roman occupation of Britain seems to have largely bypassed Llŷn. Although their main fort in North Wales was at *Segontium*, near Caernarfon, with a minor fort at Dolbenmaen, north of Criccieth, and a probable bathhouse at Tremadog, no Roman roads or other remains have been found on Llŷn itself. It seems that Llŷn was ignored as a militarily unimportant Celtic outland.

When the Romans left after four centuries of occupation, Britain was thrown to the wolves. Pictish tribes from beyond Hadrian's Wall harried northern Britain, while successive waves of Irish raiders plundered and settled parts of western Wales. Anglesey and Llŷn suffered badly, until a Celtic chieftain called Cunedda defeated the Irish in a last battle on Anglesey in 470AD. After Cunedda's death, his sons each ruled part of what would later become the kingdom of Gwynedd.

Churches and castles

By the early 6th century, Irish missionaries had converted most of the Celtic tribes in Wales to Christianity. The Welsh place name element 'llan' meant a sacred enclosure, and, later, a church. The early churches and the villages that grew up around them are often named after the priest or saint who founded them. Hence Llŷn village names such as Llanbedrog (St Pedrog's, or Peter's, church) and Llanengan (St Cian's church).

Before the conquest of Wales by Edward I, the incessant quarrelling of Welsh princes often affected the Llŷn. During the struggle for control of Gwynedd in the eleventh century, prince Gruffydd ap Cynan built an earth and timber *motte* and *bailey* castle at Nefyn. By the twelfth century, the chronicler Gerald of Wales reported that the 'sons of Owain Gwynedd' held the old Iron Age fortress on Carn Fadryn. The only Welsh castle to survive today is that at Criccieth. Much of the inner castle was built by the greatest of all Welsh princes, Llywelyn ap Iowerth, also known as 'Llywelyn Fawr' or 'Llywelyn the Great'. He was the first of the Welsh prices to unify the warring factions within Wales. Llywelyn built Criccieth about ten years before his

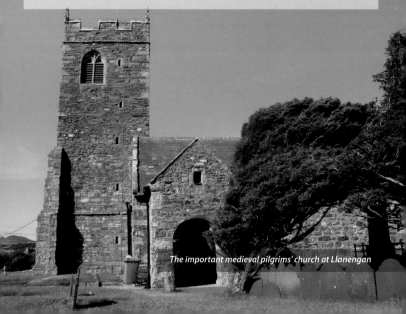

The important medieval pilgrims' church at Llanengan

Castle on the rock: *Criccieth Castle dominates the south coast of the Llŷn*

death in 1240 and used it to imprison his illegitimate eldest son, Gruffydd, in a cruel bid to stop him becoming his successor. The name Criccieth means 'prisoner's rock'.

Ironically, Gruffydd's son, also called Llywelyn, later became the last independent Prince of Wales. When he was finally killed in battle by Edward I, Edward celebrated his conquest of Wales with a grand tournament at Nefyn. To consolidate his rule, Edward then built his 'Iron Ring' of castles around North Wales at Conwy, Beaumaris, Caernarfon, Criccieth and Harlech. Criccieth was later damaged by rebels led by Owain Glyndŵr and remains a proud ruin today.

Pilgrims and herring

Once under English rule, Llŷn settled back into farming and fishing. Cattle were raised on the often boggy interior, supplemented by herring fishing during the summer. So important were the herring that they still feature in Nefyn's coat of arms, while tiny Porth Ysgaden on the north coast means the 'port of herrings'. The herring were either eaten fresh, or salted and packed into barrels for export.

The holy island of Bardsey, or Ynys Enlli, at the tip of Llŷn was a major centre of pilgrimage throughout the Middle Ages. Pilgrims streamed along established routes on both coasts, stopping at holy wells and churches along the way. In fact, the pilgrimage was so important that 12th-century Pope Callixtus II proclaimed three visits to Bardsey to be equal to one pilgrimage to Jerusalem. *(For more about the pilgrimage, see pages 76-77)*.

The sea continued to dominate the lives of Llŷn's inhabitants well into the twentieth century. Pwllheli was an important fishing and shipbuilding centre, and ships were built and repaired on the beach at Nefyn, too. The moorings at Porth Dinllaen remained an important shipping centre until the opening of Holyhead Harbour in 1873. More than 700 ships anchored in the sheltered bay during 1804. For years, the landlady of the beachside Tŷ Coch Inn kept oil lamps lit in the windows to guide ships during stormy weather.

Then the vast shoals of herring moved away, and from around 1880 the arrival of steel boats made traditional wooden shipbuilding redundant. However, when the railway reached Pwllheli in 1867, increasing numbers of summer visitors and holidaymakers flocked to Llŷn's superb beaches. Today, walkers and visitors provide an important source of extra income to this quiet and unspoilt part of Wales.

Wildlife on Llŷn

Among the many pleasures of walking the Wales Coast Path are the regular encounters with wildlife. Day by day, you'll come across a wealth of animals and plants, both common and uncommon. Much of the Llŷn Peninsula is an Area of Outstanding Natural Beauty whose unspoilt and varied habitats support a rich variety of wildlife. Keep your eyes peeled, and you've a good chance of seeing everything from wild goats, seabirds, orchids and choughs, to bottlenose dolphins, porpoise and Atlantic grey seals. Together, they add a whole new dimension to the walking experience.

Horned poppy

Atlantic grey seal

Wild goat

'Sea Pinks' or Thrift

Chough

Small copper

Western gorse and heather

Bottlenose dolphins

Manx shearwater

Ox-eye daisies

Dolphins, seals & choughs
Llŷn is a wildlife-rich Area of Outstanding Natural Beauty

Much of the rugged coast and wilder inland parts of **Llŷn** is a designated Area of Outstanding Natural Beauty. Formed in 1957, the Llŷn AONB is one of only five in Wales and covers roughly a quarter of the peninsula, or around 15,000 hectares. Its role is to protect, nurture and maintain this priceless landscape, its rich variety of habitats and the wildlife they support.

The AONB protects most of the coast between Aberdesach (roughly halfway between Caernarfon and Trefor, on the north coast) and Llanbedrog on the south coast. The AONB includes Bardsey, the smaller offshore islands and most of Llŷn's domed volcanic hills. Only the farmland of the interior and a small section of the coast around Nefyn and Morfa Nefyn is excluded.

Large parts of coastal Llŷn along the route of the Wales Coast Path are also protected as a Heritage Coastline and a European Marine Special Area of Conservation. Roughly a third of the coast is owned and cared for by the National Trust. Llŷn also boasts a National Nature Reserve, several smaller nature reserves and more than twenty Sites of Special Scientific Interest.

Unspoiled habitats

All this natural wealth depends on a happy combination of factors. Warmed by the Gulf Stream, Llŷn enjoys a mild, damp climate; snow seldom falls. Its remoteness, low population, clean air and non-intensive farming methods help make it ideal for nature, too. Llŷn's attractive patchwork of habitats includes ancient pasture, bogs and marshes, wet woodland, lowland heath and moorland, sand dunes, cliffs and offshore islands. Each of these often-threatened habitats supports its own distinctive wildlife.

Some parts of the Welsh coast have special wildlife, which can be sensitive to disturbance at certain times of the year. Seasonal restrictions to access may be needed in order to protect sensitive plants and animals. Please help look after Welsh wildlife by complying with instructions on any signs asking you to keep dogs on leads or to avoid particular areas at particular times.

Sheep farming still dominates the peninsula's agriculture, and drystone walls, hedges and earthen banks, characteristically frame Llŷn's small fields. In spring and early summer the roadside banks and narrow country lanes are decked with wildflowers; look for primroses, violets, celandines, bluebells and cowslips, followed later by pink campion, cow parsley, foxgloves, gorse and fragrant honeysuckle.

Atlantic grey seals 'haul out' on rocks below Trwyn Porth Dinllaen, near Nefyn

Rare birds: *Llŷn's unspoilt coast supports as many as 60 breeding pairs of choughs*

Coastal heath

Perhaps the most iconic of Llŷn's habitats is its seemingly wild coastal heathland. Dominated by heather and low-growing western gorse, the heathland is ablaze with yellow and purple in late summer, when the heather is in full bloom. Wiry moor grasses edge paths and open areas; while tall spires of foxgloves and occasional young rowan trees add a vertical element to the scene. Superb examples of this beautiful habitat can be explored around the tip of Llŷn, on Mynydd Anelog, Mynydd Mawr and Pen y Cil. There's a particularly lovely, elevated section between Mynydd Penarfynydd and Mynydd y Graig, near Rhiw. And don't miss the open heathland and common land on Mynydd Cilan, at the eastern end of Hell's Mouth. These apparently 'unspoiled' heaths are actually very carefully managed by the National Trust in close partnership with tenant farmers.

This increasingly threatened yet beautiful habitat supports a mixture of unusual plants and animals. Key species to look out for include peregrines, choughs, stonechats, brown hares, common lizards and adders.

Along the coast, spring and early summer brings a flush of maritime wildflowers. There are pale primroses everywhere on the grassy cliffs, mixed with sky blue squill. Later come mixed drifts of vibrant sea pinks, wild thyme and coastal bluebells. By full summer, the 'unimproved' grassy margins alongside the clifftop Wales Coast Path are bright with wildflowers. Look for yarrow, knapweed, rockrose, hawksbit and ladies bedstraw amid the grasses. The earth and stone field banks, or *clawdd*, are home to brambles, wind-trimmed gorse and hawthorn, wild thyme, common and kidney vetches, wild carrot and devil's bit scabious.

Where tiny streams and waterfalls cleave the clifftop, lush water loving plants fill the clefts and valleys. Here sedge, meadowsweet, alexanders, yellow flag iris, watercress and pungent water mint fringe the water.

Birds and butterflies

In summer, the clifftop grasslands are alive with insects, too. Listen for the tick of grasshoppers amid the stems. Unexpected numbers of butterflies pirouette above the grass; watch out for small whites, meadow browns, gatekeepers, common blues, small coppers, and the occasional skipper.

Typical clifftop birds include the ever-present rock pipit, skylarks, linnets and stonechats. Kestrels hunt and hover over the grass. And, all summer long, swallows and martins swoop and turn low over the grassy cliffs hawking for flies. A large colony of sand martins nest in holes in the sandy cliffs near the Tŷ Coch Inn, at Porth Dinllaen.

Yellow gorse and purple heather colour the common on Mynydd Cilan

Rocky coasts

The flat rocks and pebbly shore below the path are often busy with gulls, shags and cormorants, oystercatchers and ringed plovers, with occasional terns fishing just offshore.

Llŷn's higher cliffs and islands provide important nesting sites for sea-going birds such as kittiwakes, fulmars, herring gulls, lesser- and great black-backed gulls, guillemots and razorbills.

The coastal cliffs also provide hunting grounds for ravens, kestrels and peregrines. Clifftops are a favourite feeding ground for Llŷn's iconic choughs; up to five percent of the British breeding population are found on the Llŷn Peninsula. Look out for these aerobatic red-billed crows at the rocky tip of Llŷn — especially around Mynydd Anelog, Mynydd Mawr, Pen y Cil, Mynydd Penarfynnydd, Mynydd y Graig and Mynydd Cilan.

Bardsey island is an internationally-important summer haven for nesting Manx shearwaters, while the Ynysoedd Gwylan (or Gull Islands), off Aberdaron, support nesting puffins. This 'Land's End' of Wales is also the first landfall for small birds on their annual migrations, and Bardsey is an important bird observatory and ringing station. Around 100 different species of birds are ringed annually on Bardsey.

Bottlenose dolphins

Watching you: *Curious Atlantic grey seals often watch walkers from just offshore*

Grey seals and dolphins

As well as warming the land, the Gulf Stream brings nutrients that sustain a rich marine environment. In summer, the warm currents bring shoals of sand eels close to shore. As well as being the staple diet of seabirds such as puffins, they are preyed on by shoals of mackerel, which are eaten in turn by other marine animals such a grey seals, porpoise and dolphins.

Large breeding colonies of Atlantic grey seals can be found on Bardsey and St Tudwal's islands, off Abersoch. Smaller groups live along the northern coast and can often be spotted, staring, doglike, at walkers from close inshore, or 'hauled out' onto the rocks at low tide, especially at places such as the Carreg Ddu rocks, off Porth Dinllaen, near Nefyn.

Porpoise, dolphins and other marine mammals are often seen around Llŷn. If it's very close to the shore, it's probably a porpoise. Often seen from both headlands and coastal cruises, particularly off Abersoch, are bottlenose dolphins, sometimes in pods of up to twenty or so. One of the best places to see dolphins from land is from the headlands on Mynydd Rhiw, Mynydd Cilan or Trwyn yr Wylfa, on Llŷn's southwest coast. Common dolphins, harbour dolphins and Risso's dolphins are occasionally seen farther out, feeding in the tidal currents towards Bardsey. Boatmen sometimes report both minke and pilot whales in deep water around Llŷn, too.

Day Sections

The **Llŷn Peninsula**
section of the
Wales Coast Path

Sunset over Bardsey, or Ynys Enlli (Day Section 5)

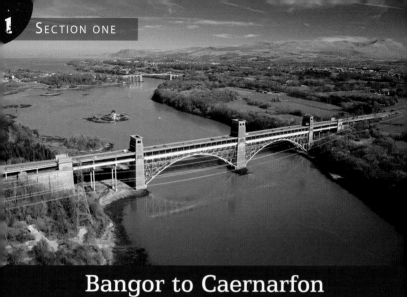

Bangor to Caernarfon

Distance: *12½miles/ 20 kilometres* | **Start:** *Bangor Pier, Bangor SH 585 732*
Finish: *Caernarfon SH 477 626* | **Maps:** *OS Landranger 115 Snowdon & Caernarfon + 123 Llŷn Peninsula; and OS Explorer 263 Anglesey East + 254 Llŷn Peninsula East*

Outline: A flat yet varied Day Section alongside the tidal Menai Strait to the walled town of Caernarfon and its spectacular medieval castle.

The initial stretch along Menai's wooded shores passes the Menai Suspension Bridge, the tidal 'Swellies' and Pont Britannia, before looping through the Vaynol Estate. The route then follows the Lôn Las cycleway and recreational route that runs roughly parallel with the Strait, passes the Plas Menai National Watersports Centre, and continues to the walled town of Caernarfon and its stunning medieval castle — now recognised as a World Heritage Site.

Services: *Bangor is a busy university city with lots of accommodation, banks, post offices, shops, pubs and bars, restaurants, cafés and takeaways. Cathedral, museum and pier. Public toilets by pier. Pubs and cafés en-route, near Menai Suspension Bridge and Y Felinheli. Caernarfon TIC 01286 672232 | caernarfon.tic@gwynedd.gov.uk. Chubbs Cabs 01248 353535*

Don't miss: Bangor Pier – a classic Edwardian seaside pier | **Menai's two iconic bridges** – both engineering wonders of their day | **Caernarfon's Victoria Dock** – marina, pier, modern gallery and restaurant

▲ *The Menai Strait with the Britannia Bridge*

Bangor

Bangor is a small coastal city on the Menai Strait overlooking the Isle of Anglesey. Centred on the ancient cathedral and university, the old city slopes in a maze of streets down to the pretty eastern end of the Menai Strait where refurbished Victorian Bangor Pier reaches out towards Anglesey. The view from the pier embraces the Great Orme, Llandudno, Snowdonia, Anglesey and, looking westwards along the Strait, Telford's iconic suspension bridge. You couldn't pick a better place to start this lovely section of the Wales Coast Path.

Bangor takes its name from the old Welsh word for the wattle fence that surrounded early Christian sites. The Celtic Christian Saint Deiniol founded a monastery here in AD 550, and the present cathedral was built on the same site between 1496 and 1532. Throughout the Middle Ages, the cathedral was a spiritual centre for the independent principality of Gwynedd, and the tomb of the Welsh resistance fighter, Owain Gwynedd, can still be seen in the cathedral today. So it's no surprise that Bangor was the gathering point for medieval pilgrims starting out on the arduous journey to Ynys Enlli, or Bardsey, the 'island of 20,000 saints' at the very tip of Llŷn.

Looking towards Porth Penrhyn from Bangor Pier

The route: **Bangor to Caernarfon**

1 This section of the Wales Coast Path begins at **Bangor Pier**, near Garth, at Bangor's most northern point. Here, the cast iron and timber Bangor Pier reaches almost halfway across the **Menai Strait** towards the Isle of Anglesey's wooded shores. It's a delightful spot.

Be sure to walk out onto the pier, whose onion domes, ornate shelters and pier-end tearoom all evoke Bangor's Edwardian hey-day as a seaside resort. There's a small fee, and ample parking and toilets nearby.

From the pier, return to the corner opposite the '**Tap and Spile**' pub above, and turn right, gently uphill on the quiet coast road. Within 500 metres, it narrows to a one-way section with adjacent cycle path. To continue on the main official route, walk ahead (to the left) on the gently rising road.

Alternative route: *A pretty low-tide short cut along the Menai shore*
Take the righthand fork here and drop down the narrow, tree-shaded lane to a boatyard. Turn left past sheds and moored boats. The path skirts the isolated **Old Bath House** to continue easily along the rocky shore for 500 metres to a large white house on the water's edge.

The **official route** continues uphill on the quiet road, veering away from the shore above a meadow with a **modern stone circle** *erected to celebrate the 1931 National Eisteddfod in Bangor*. A few hundred metres later, the path

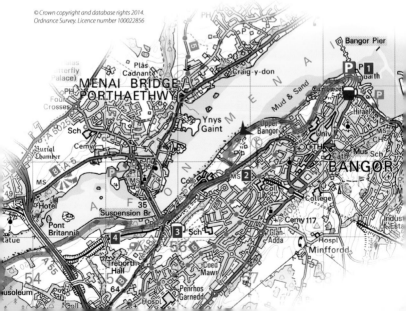

© Crown copyright and database rights 2014.
Ordnance Survey. Licence number 100022856

Along the shore: *Bangor Pier seen from the Menai Strait*

kinks through a gap in the wall to follow a tarmac path along the upper edge of the field. Beyond the field, go right along the pavement for 400 metres, then turn right down signposted **Gorad Road**. Go straight ahead at the crossroads and head down the shaded lane ahead. The tarmac lane drops steeply beneath trees to emerge above a shingly beach.

Immediately above the shore, turn left and go through the signposted wooden footgate. Follow the field edge uphill to the right above the **white waterside house**. Keep to the field edge as it curves around to the left, to go through the kissing gate in the far, top righthand corner of the field.

For the next ½ mile/1 kilometre or so, the path runs through the lovely, ancient mixed woodland of the North Wales Wildlife Trust's '**Nant Porth Nature Reserve**'. The undulating path traverses the dappled slopes with views of the Strait below. Ignore faint paths down to the water, eventually climbing timber-edged steps to a ruined barn and kissing gate into fields at the top of the woods.

From here, a fenced path zig-zags around the periphery of several pastures to emerge at a metal kissing gate onto a tarmaced drive. Turn left and then right onto a narrow lane to emerge at a roundabout on the A5 beside the entrance to **Bangor City Football Club**.

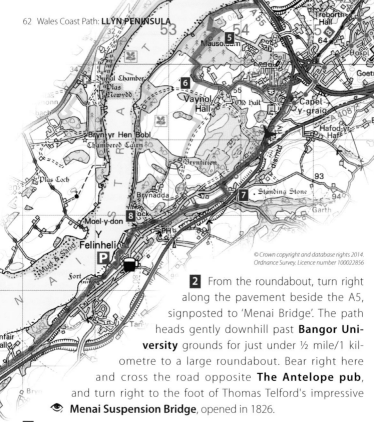

© Crown copyright and database rights 2014.
Ordnance Survey. Licence number 100022856

2 From the roundabout, turn right along the pavement beside the A5, signposted to 'Menai Bridge'. The path heads gently downhill past **Bangor University** grounds for just under ½ mile/1 kilometre to a large roundabout. Bear right here and cross the road opposite **The Antelope pub**, and turn right to the foot of Thomas Telford's impressive ◆ **Menai Suspension Bridge**, opened in 1826.

3 A three-way Wales Coast Path signpost here points across the bridge to 'Ynys Môn/Isle of Anglesey' for the circuit of the island. But to continue on this section, walk beneath the arches of the bridge's massive anchor house; on the far side, another signpost points on along the road above the Strait. Pass the entrance to 'Ceris Newydd' nursing home on the right, and continue ahead on the road into **Treborth Business Park**. Pass the business units on the left keeping ahead along the road, soon passing between old stone gate pillars into **Treborth Botanic Gardens**.

4 A little farther on, look for the signed coast path on the right. Leave the road here, turning right onto a gravel path into the woods. The footpath swings left as you approach the Strait, to pass **Paxton's Cascade** — a small waterfall that tumbles into the sea.

A good path heads through the woods, with the Strait down to your right. Depending on the state of the tide you will be able to both see and hear the famous '**Swellies**' as you move through the trees.

Wild water: *Ynys Gored Goch crouches in the heart of the dramatic 'Swellies' tide race*

The Swellies is an impressive tide race that courses through the narrowest part of the Strait that divides Anglesey from the mainland, between the two bridges. At the highest point of the tide, look out for the apparent 'step' in the water where the sea plunges over a rocky ledge.

After a section of **boardwalk** the footpath forks. Keep ahead to the right, passing beneath the approach spans of Robert Stephenson's massive **Pont Britannia** bridge, *opened in 1850 and built originally to carry the railway through massive 'tubes' onto Anglesey. The original structure was damaged by fire in 1970 and extensively rebuilt.* At a concrete road, go ahead past a section of the original bridge removed after the fire damage in 1970. Take the gravel path ahead into the trees. Beyond a small gate, the path swings right to continue through woods above the shore.

5 Farther on, a metal gate in a high stone wall leads into the National Trust woods at '**Glan Faenol**'. *This beautiful section of the Menai Strait was acquired by the Trust in 1985 as part of the larger Vaynol Estate. The purchase was prompted in part by a desire to protect the scenic views from the National Trust's Plas Newydd Estate on the Anglesey shore, across the Strait.*

At a T-junction with a gravel path, turn left. The path soon curves to the right, passing a neglected, spooky **mausoleum**. Follow the track ahead here, eventually reaching the edge of the woods. Turn left with the track and follow the edge of fields, keeping the woods on your left. *(At the time of writing, there are plans to extend the coast path along the Menai Strait to Y Felinheli.)*

6 At the end of the woods, go through a kissing gate on the left and walk up to a picnic area and car park. Go through the car park and on along the access track. Follow the track past **Vaynol Hall**, where it becomes a tarmac road.

The **Vaynol Estate** *was once the property of the wealthy Assheton-Smith family, who made their money from the North Wales' slate quarries. Now a premier outdoor venue, the park has hosted events such as the* Bryn Terfel's Faenol Festival, *the* National Eisteddfod *and* BBC Radio 1's 'Big Weekend'.

Continue along the road through the **Menai Business Park** to a T-junction at the end of **Ffordd y Plas**. Turn right along the road and go ahead at a mini roundabout passing the **Premier Inn** and '**Parc Britannia**' pub to reach the main roundabout on the A487.

Turn right here, following the main **A487 Caernarfon road**. Cross over where the pavement ends beside the old access road to the estate and follow the pavement/cycleway downhill on the opposite side. Cross over once more immediately before the roundabout, passing the **Vaynol Estate gates** on the right. Around 250 metres later, cross to the lefthand side of road again. Then, some 300 metres farther on, take the road on the left signposted to 'Llanberis'.

7 Just before the lane passes beneath the expressway, turn right into a lane signed to 'Siloh'. Within the next 300 metres, look for **Lôn Las Menai** (a recreational route and cycleway) that veers away from the lane on the right. The sign reads 'Lôn Las Menai – Caernarfon 4'.

It's good to be away from the traffic; and the recreational route is easy to follow. Ignore a righthand fork, and continue ahead. Within 750 metres bear right (as signed for 'Cycleway 8') down

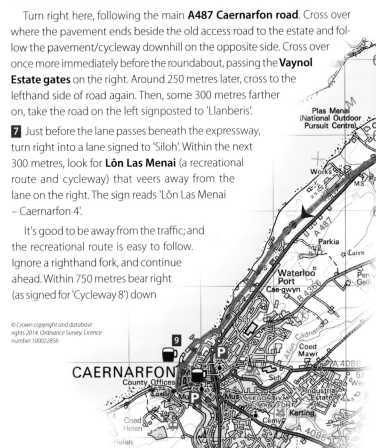

Strait's sunset: *Two canoeists enjoy an evening paddle below Menai's famous Pont Britannia*

to the road. Cross the road, turn left along the pavement and then, almost immediately, bear right down the road. This leads down past the little dock at **Y Felinheli**.

8 Follow the road ahead through a housing development. Before you reach the end of the road, look for the signed coast path and cycleway that passes between apartment blocks on the left. At the road, turn right and follow it as it swings left past the **Garddfon Inn** and on along the waterfront.

Follow the road past the **sailing club**, through a small industrial estate then steeply up the hill. Immediately after the new health centre, bear right onto the Lôn Las Menai again. The next section of the path follows **Lôn Las Menai** all the way to Caernarfon — around 2½ miles/ 4 kilometres — joining the road briefly at one point. It's straightforward and direct and brings you out beside new apartment blocks around **Caernarfon docks**.

9 Keep to the right of the high-rise apartments to reach busy **Victoria Dock** with its yachts and waterside cafés, gift shops and gallery. Bear left, then right, around the dock crossing the footbridge. At the far end turn right, then bear left along the **waterside promenade** below the **town walls**. This Day Section finishes below the imposing walls of **Caernarfon Castle** immediately before the swing bridge over **Afon Seiont**. The town, shops and **Tourist Information Centre** are through the gatehouse on the left.

Caernarfon Castle

Edward I's 'Iron Ring'

Wales has more castles for its size than any other country in the world

Of all Wales' 400 or so historic castles, the most formidable and impressive are undoubtedly the 'Iron Ring' of fortresses built by Edward I to encircle Gwynedd in North Wales — the last bastion of Welsh resistance to the hated English overlords.

From the Norman conquest onwards, a series of charismatic Welsh leaders had fought against English dominion. Eventually, in 1267 the weak English king, Henry III was forced to sign the Treaty of

Montgomery, recognising Llywelyn ap Gruffydd as the first Prince of Wales. Yet the autonomy of Wales was short-lived.

Henry's ruthless son, Edward I, was made of far sterner stuff. After his first successful military campaign against the Welsh in 1277, he strengthened and rebuilt his father's old castles in

Conwy Castle

North Wales. Following Llywelyn's second but unsuccessful uprising and death in 1282, Edward was determined to finish the fight. His 'Iron Ring' of mighty fortresses at Conwy, Caernarfon, Beaumaris and Harlech encircled Snowdonia. Welsh resistance was effectively crushed. Together, the castles of Edward's 'Iron Ring' represent Europe's most expensive and ambitious medieval military building project.

Harlech Castle

The new castles were the work of Master James of St George, the top military architect of his day. Unlike earlier, simple square castles, Edward's new fortresses had inner and outer curtain walls and circular towers and gateways. They show a clever progression towards the highly evolved concentric designs of Harlech and Beaumaris.

Their design was based on the *bastide* towns of Gascony in southwest France whose castles were integrated into walled towns. Populated exclusively by English settlers, these new market towns cunningly engaged the Welsh in English ways. The Welsh were allowed to enter the towns by day but kept out at night.

> **"Beaumaris, Conwy, Caernarfon and Harlech are the finest examples of late 13th- and early 14th century military architecture in Europe."**
>
> *UNESCO statement of significance, 2013*

When they were new, the castles were boldly whitewashed to emphasise their power. Part of a clever overall project, they occupied key strategic positions, were a day's march apart, and could be resupplied by sea.

Today, many of these iconic castles are cared for by Cadw: Welsh Historic Monuments. Conwy, Caernarfon, Beaumaris and Harlech are also internationally renowned and protected by UNESCO as World Heritage Sites. All of them are open to the public and together they give a fascinating insight into Wales' turbulent past.

More information: Caernarfon Castle: Open daily, except 24, 25, 26 December and New Year's Day. 01286 677617

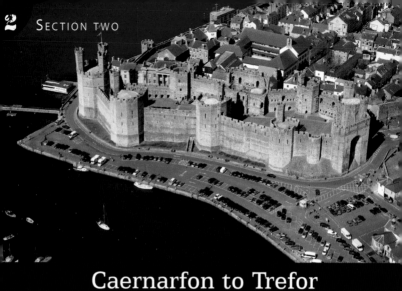

Caernarfon to Trefor

Distance: *17½ miles / 28 kilometres* | **Start:** *Caernarfon Castle (Afon Seiont) SH 477 626*
Finish: *Trefor Harbour SH 376 473* | **Maps:** *OS Landranger 115 Snowdon & Caernarfon + 123 Llŷn Peninsula; and OS Explorer 263 Anglesey East + 254 Llŷn Peninsula East*

Outline: A walk of two halves: quiet lanes beside the Menai Strait to Dinas Dinlle, followed by a roadside hike to Clynnog Fawr and Trefor.

From the walled town of Caernarfon, the path crosses the Afon Seiont before tracing the flat and increasingly open coast past Foryd Bay Nature Reserve. Beyond tiny Caernarfon Airport and Dinas Dinlle hillfort, the official route heads inland before following roadside pavements along the A499 to Clynnog Fawr and the tiny harbour settlement at Trefor. Don't miss the important pilgrims' church at Clynnog Fawr. Nonetheless, some walkers may choose to take a bus or taxi for all or part of this Day Section, or it could be cycled.

Services: *The walled town of Caernarfon has plenty of accommodation, banks, post office, shops, pubs, restaurants, cafés and takeaways. Saturday market. Public toilets. Caernarfon TIC 01286 672232 | caernarfon.tic@gwynedd.gov.uk. Café, shop and takeaway at Dinas Dinlle. Short detour to Harp Inn pub at Llandwrog. Café at Glynllifon Country Park. Garage and shop at Clynnog Fawr. Shop and post office at Trefor. M&R Taxis 01286 831867*

👁 **Don't miss: Caernarfon Castle** – one of the finest medieval castles in Wales | **Dinas Dinlle** – Iron Age hillfort overlooking the sea | **St Beuno's, Clynnog Fawr** – large, important church on the medieval Pilgrims' Trail to Bardsey

▲ *Caernarfon Castle from the air*

Caernarfon

Caernarfon is a busy medieval walled town overlooking the eastern end of the Menai Strait, dominated by its World Heritage status castle. The town is a major tourist centre with a busy harbour and marina and a good range of shops, hotels, restaurants, pubs and cafés. It's also the start of the dramatic Welsh Highland Railway that runs into the heart of Snowdonia.

Backed by mountains and with abundant natural resources nearby, Caernarfon occupies an established strategic site on the coastal plain where the Afon Seiont flows into the Menai Strait. It was probably a special place long before the Romans defeated the local *Ordovices* tribe and built their fort of *Segontium* here on the hill above the town, in AD 79.

So, when the 13th-century English king, Edward I, decided to build his 'Iron Ring' of castles around North Wales to subjugate the Welsh, this was an obvious site. Caernarfon was made a borough and market town in 1284, and was later represented by Lloyd-George, the fiery Welsh politician and First World War British Prime Minister. Caernarfon was granted 'Royal Town' status in 1974. Today, Caernarfon has expanded beyond its medieval walls and is the seat of Gwynedd County Council.

Caernarfon Castle guards the strategic southern end of the Menai Strait

Coastal fortress: *Edward I's castle at Caernarfon dominates the little harbour*

The route: **Caernarfon to Trefor**

1 Immediately below the imposing walls of 👁 **Caernarfon Castle**, cross the modern swing bridge that spans the mouth of **Afon Seoint** where it opens into the Menai Strait. On the far side, turn right and walk along the pavement as the road swings left along the coast.

Follow this quiet road above the open shore, past a **country park** and a **golf club**, for 1½ miles/ 2.5 kilometres or so until it curves inland around the vast tidal inlet of **Foryd Bay**.

Across the bay is Fort Belan, immediately opposite Abemenai Point on the Anglesey shore. It was built in 1775 during the American War of Independence to protect the entrance to the Menai Strait from American privateers. Today, the unique Grade 1 listed buildings can be rented as a holiday home.

Detour: *To the tiny medieval church of St Baglan's*
A short footpath leads across the fields to St Baglan's Church. *Alone in the fields, the disued church is cared for by the eccentrically named UK charity, 'Friends of Friendless Churches'. Cadw have given the church*

Grade 1 listed building status for its unspoilt medieval interior and evocative 18th-century pews.

2 Half a mile/1 kilometre later, the road bends sharply to the left, away from the shore, to skirt the reedy mouth of **Afon Gwyrfai**. Continue ahead for around ½ mile/1 kilometre to a T-junction and turn right towards the tiny hamlet of **Saron**. Cross the bridge over the Afon Gwyrfai and take the next lane on the right just beyond Saron. Follow the lane as it curves to the left

Strategic Site?

Caernarfon Castle commands a strategic position first occupied by the Roman fort of Segontium and then by a Norman motte and bailey castle. Situated on the north bank of Afon Seiont where it flows into the Menai Strait, the site controls north-south access along the coastal plain, the vital crossing to Anglesey — the 'bread basket of Wales' — and the ancient sea route between Wales and Ireland. Caernarfon's Welsh name refers back to the Roman 'caer' or 'fortress in Arfon'.

Ancient worship: *Tiny St Baglan's church is lost in the fields overlooking Abermenai Point*

and runs alongside **Y Foryd Coastal Nature Reserve**, whose wooden bird hide looks out over brackish pools and open saltmarsh. The road soon turns inland again, for almost ½ mile/1 kilometre, to reach **Blythe Farm**. Just before the farm, look for a Wales Coast Path signpost pointing to the right, off the road, down a tree-fringed drive signed for 'Chatham'.

Past a house, the path follows a green lane through a low, windswept wood to emerge on reclaimed farmland at the tip of **Foryd Bay**.

Now a Local Nature Reserve, Foryd Bay's 250 hectares of intertidal mud and saltmarsh support huge numbers of native and migratory wildfowl and waders. In the 9th century, the bay was a favourite shelter for Viking longboats.

A short, raised causeway leads over a wooden footbridge across the narrow **Afon Carrog** and up onto a vast flood defence embankment that curves away on either side along the western flank of Foryd Bay. Turn right and walk along the top of the embankment, high above the fields and saltmarsh. When the embankment reaches the corner of a large static caravan site, or holiday park, roughly 800 metres later, turn left, through a kissing gate, onto a broad track signposted for the Wales Coast Path.

3 Walk past the entrance to '**Morfa Lodge Holiday Park**' and continue straight ahead along the tarmac, for 1 mile/ 1.5 kilometres, past **Caernarfon**

Airport and the adjacent **Airworld Aviation Museum**. When the road reaches the sand and shingle shore and car park at **Morfa Dinlle**, turn left and continue along the raised path that skirts the stony shore of Caernarfon Bay to a cluster of shops below the striking mound of 👁 **Dinas Dinlle**, crowned by an **Iron Age hillfort**.

Dinas Dinlle is a small beachside community with a handful of amenities centred around an Iron Age hillfort on a glacial hillock. The huge sand and pebble beach is protected as a Site of Special Scientific Interest for its internationally important glacial deposits from the last Ice Age, now exposed in the sea-eroded cliffs.

In Welsh legend, the hillfort is linked with one of the heroes of the Mabinogion, *Lleu Llaw Gyffes. It seems Dinas Dinlle's name comes from the old Welsh meaning 'the fort or settlement of Lleu'.*

The sense of space on this other-wise open coast is exhilarating,

Prehistoric stronghold: *Ancient Dinas Dinlle hillfort has been badly eroded by the sea*

especially from the hillfort's breezy summit — with striking views towards Bwlch Mawr, Gyrn Ddu, Gyrn Goch and Yr Eifl and beyond, down the full length of the Llŷn Peninsula.

Detour: *Short walk to a picturesque village, church and pub*
To visit the picturesque village of **Llandwrog** with its grand Victorian **St Twrog's church** and friendly local pub, the **Harp Inn**, take the lefthand fork here. The Harp Inn has a bar, games room, beer garden, restaurant and accommodation. It's under ½ mile/ 1 kilometre away.

4 Otherwise, to keep to the **official route**, follow the lanes out towards the main road, keeping to the right when the road forks.

5 At the main **A499**, cross over and turn right along the pavement.

(**Note**: From here, with only a few short off-road sections and occasional suggested alternative routes, the official coast path runs alongside the main road for the next 6½ mile/ 9 kilometres until it reaches Trefor. Although the pavement is often separated from the road by a broad grassy verge, and is both safe and walkable, some walkers may prefer to catch a bus or taxi to Trefor.

The coast path runs alongside the main road. At first the path is flanked on the left by the high stone wall of the **Glynllifon estate**. *Now an agricultural college and country park, it was once the home of the local Glyn family, who* *later became the Wynns by marriage. In 1776, Sir Thomas Wynn was given a peerage to become Lord Newborough. Today, Parc Glynllifon's 70 acres of exotic trees and plants are cared for by Gwynedd County Council with the help of Natural Resources Wales, Cadw and Welsh Historic Gardens.*

Just over 1 mile/ 1.5 kilometres later, turn off the main road to the left, onto a short stretch of the old road flanked by cottages that runs parallel to the modern A499.

The path soon returns to the side of the main road. When it crosses the **Afon Llyfni**, some 500 metres later, continue through **Pontllyfni**, passing a garage on the right.

Alternative route: *Avoiding the main road on the next stretch*

Cross the road immediately after the garage, and turn right down a narrow lane edged by bungalows and a caravan park, which slopes down to the shore. Close to the water's edge, turn left

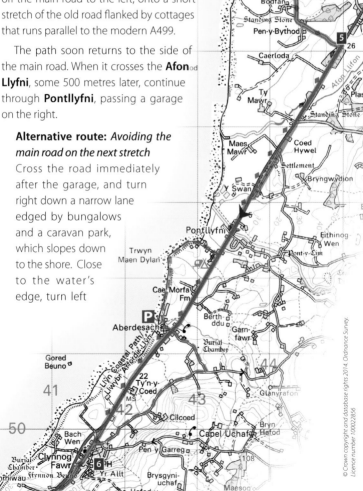

© Crown copyright and database rights 2014 Ordnance Survey. Licence number 10002856

St Beuno's Church, Clynnog Fawr

Pilgrim Paths to Bardsey

Medieval pilgrims streamed towards Bardsey, the 'Island of 20,000 Saints'

Bardsey, or Ynys Enlli, at the western tip of Llŷn, was one of the best known goals for pilgrims in medieval Britain. There had been a monastery on the island for almost a thousand years — from the sixth to the sixteenth century. Like many of the ancient churches on Llŷn, it was part of a distinctive Celtic Christian tradition stretching back to the early Irish missionaries.

Several sources confirm Bardsey's importance as a centre of pilgrimage. Twelfth-century Pope Callixtus II proclaimed that three pilgrimages to Bardsey were equal to one to the holy city of Jerusalem, while the medieval writer and avid recruiter for the Third Crusade, Gerald of Wales, mentioned the huge numbers of pilgrims already heading for Bardsey in 1188.

St Beuno's Church, Pistyll

Many of those making the long and arduous journey came from all over Britain. They were hoping for a miracle cure or, at worst, to die either on Bardsey or on the way there. Hospices and even hospice fields (where the sick and dying could be cared for by local people for a fee) sprang up near many of the churches. Most pilgrims believed that to die on Bardsey, or on en route, guaranteed them a place in Heaven.

Two Pilgrim Paths headed for Bardsey along the length of Llŷn. One traced the north coast and the other, the south coast. Walkers and modern pilgrims can still follow both routes today, stopping off at churches, crosses, holy wells and other ancient sites along the way. Most are either actually on or within easy walking distance of the Wales Coast Path.

St Hywyn's Church, Aberdaron

> *"So priketh hem nature in hir corages, Than longen folk to go on pilgrimages."*
>
> *'Canterbury Tales', 14th century*

Pilgrims on the **northern route** gathered as far away as Bangor Cathedral but most started from St Beuno's church at Clynnog Fawr.

The next stop was St Aelhaearn's church at Llanaelhaearn, followed by isolated St Beuno's church perched above the sea at Pistyll, and the double-naved St Gwynhoedl's church at Llangwnnadl. The final church and resting place for pilgrims before the perilous crossing to Bardsey itself was St Hywyn's at Aberdaron.

Pilgrims on the **southern route** mustered at the ancient twin-chambered healing well at St Cybi's Well, inland from Criccieth. The next stop was St Cawrdraf's church at Abererch, near Pwllheli. Then came the simple coastal chapel of St Pedrog's, at Llanbedrog, followed by St Einion's at Llanengan, not far inland behind Porth Neigwl (or Hell's Mouth). As on the northern route, the final church on the Pilgrims' Path to Bardsey was St Hywyn's at Aberdaron.

More information: Many of Llŷn's pilgrimage churches have introductory booklets or information sheets. Some also have exhibitions or church shops.

on a signposted footpath through the caravan park to the rocky shore of Caernarfon Bay. The path traces the rocky shore below low, boulder clay cliffs around **Trwyn Maen Dylan** to the tiny seaside settlement of **Aberdesach**. Cross the footbridge over the **Afon Desach** and follow the lane between the houses back to the main road.

Cross over and follow the lane ahead gently uphill, away from the coast. Look out for **Dolmen Bachwen**, a Neolithic burial chamber, in a field on the left, half way up the hill.

At the T-junction at the top of the slope, turn right and follow the lane running almost parallel with the main road, gently downhill now into **Clynnog Fawr**.

To stay on the **official route**, beyond **Pontllyfni** continue alongside the A499 for another 1½ miles/ 2 kilometres to the ancient village, church and holy well at 👁 **Clynnog Fawr**.

Clynnog Fawr is notable for its large and important pilgrims' church. Strategically located at the northern end of the pass linking the two coasts on either side of Llŷn, Clynnog Fawr was chosen by the Celtic missionary Saint Beuno as the site of his religious foundation, or clas — a cross between a college and a monastery — around 630 AD. In old Welsh, Clynnog means 'the place of holly trees'.

Saint Beuno was widely reputed to have miraculous healing powers. In one legend, he reattached the head of a decapitated woman. It's said that a well, or 'holy spring', promptly sprang up on the spot where she was resurrected. Known today as 'St Beuno's Well', it can still be seen today behind an iron gate along the old road — now a cycleway — just south of the village.

After his death, the collegiate church became a gathering

Pilgrims' trail: *Saint Beuno's Church, Clynnog Fawr*

place for pilgrims setting out for the holy island of Bardsey, or Ynys Enlli, at the tip of Llŷn. Later burnt down by both Vikings and Normans, the church was rebuilt in Perpendicular style in the 16th century. Inside are a 16th century chancel screen and choir stalls and a huge alms chest — the Cyff Beuno — carved from a single ash tree. Outside in the churchyard are Maen Beuno, *or 'St Beuno's Stone', and a prehistoric standing stone carved with a Saxon sundial sometime in the 10th century. For many thousands of years this has been a sacred place.*

6 The coast path follows the road out of the village. Take the cycleway ahead when the road swings to the right towards the main A499. The cycleway — which was once the old road — passes above the main road to join it around 500 metres later. Continue on the paved path/cycleway through the hamlet of **Gyrn Goch** and continue for the next 1¾ miles/ 3 kilometres.

7 Cross the road and take the lane signed to '**Trefor**'. Turn right as you enter the village and follow the signed lane that leads down to the **car park** and **public toilets** just above **Trefor Harbour** where this Day Section ends.

Trefor to Nefyn

Distance: *9¼ miles/ 15 kilometres* | **Start:** *Trefor Harbour SH 376 473*
Finish: *Nefyn (village centre) SH 307 405* | **Maps:** *OS Landranger 115 Snowdon & Caernarfon + 123 Llŷn Peninsula; and OS Explorer 254 Llŷn Peninsula East*

Outline: Dramatic, atmospheric and varied, this is the most demanding yet also one of the most rewarding Day Sections on the Llŷn coast path.

The route leaves the distinctive Welsh quarrying village of Trefor before climbing steeply over Yr Eifl. From the pass at the top, a vast panorama opens out across the Irish Sea and ahead to Bardsey at the tip of Llŷn. Then the path plunges into the hidden valley of Nant Gwrtheyrn with its legends, quarry ruins and Welsh Language Centre. Back on the clifftop, the path drops steadily past the ancient pilgrim's church at Pistyll and on along the coast to the small seaside town of Nefyn.

Services: *Village shop and post office in Trefor. Toilets near Trefor harbour. Café, bar and licensed restaurant at Nant Gwrtheyrn. Detour to Llithfaen's community shop and pub. Nefyn has full range of facilities from accommodation, supermarkets, cafés, chip shop, post office and bank to doctor's surgery, phamacy and library. Nefyn Taxi Service 01758 720131*

👁 **Don't miss:** | **Nant Gwrtheyrn** – Welsh Language Centre, café, bar and heritage centre | **Tre'r Ceiri** – stunning prehistoric hillfort | **St Beuno's Church, Pistyll** - atmospheric medieval pilgrim's church

▲ *On the cliffs at Trwyn y Tâl, Trefor*

Trefor

Trefor is a distinctive, tight-knit Welsh-speaking community tucked below the foot of Yr Eifl — Llŷn's distinctive, triple-peaked hills. Although Trefor means 'sea town' in Welsh, the village owes its existence to the vast granite quarries that scar the north face of the hills above. In its Victorian heyday, the small harbour with its pier was busy with ships exporting granite road setts and kerbs around the world. Today the pier is popular with sea anglers, while the inner harbour shelters mainly leisure craft. Look out for grey seals, too; a large colony thrives along this quiet and craggy coast.

Trefor Harbour once exported granite road 'setts' around Britain

Secluded shore: *Beyond Trefor the pebbly beach is overshadowed by Yr Eifl*

The route: **Trefor to Nefyn**

1 From the car park and public toilets follow the road towards **Trefor Harbour**. To the left of the harbour and pier is a little beach; go through the gate by the breakwater here and follow the gravel road ahead. This soon crosses a footbridge and a little farther on swings left. Bear right here through a kissing gate that leads onto **Morfa**, a rocky headland owned by the National Trust. The path zig-zags up the bank ahead, then continues along the top of the sea cliffs of **Trwyn y Tâl** with the 300 metre (1,000-foot) cliffs of **Yr Eifl** rising impressively ahead.

Yr Eifl, whose name means the 'trident' in Welsh, rises abruptly from the rocky coastline. This iconic mountain comprises the triple peaks of Tre'r Ceiri (485 metres), Garn Ganol (564 metres) and Garn Fawr (444 metres). Rich with history and wildlife, it's the symbolic gateway to the Welsh cultural stronghold of Llŷn.

2 Continue on the grassy cliff top path until you reach a stony cove where there is a **cottage** in the fields over to the left and a kissing gate. Go through the kissing gate and walk to a path junction. Access to the beach is on the right here; otherwise, turn left along the path to reach the access drive to the cottage of '**West End**'. Turn right along the drive and follow it past the front of the cottage. Stay with the driveway as it turns left, away from the sea, and rises to a second house. Immediately before the house, turn sharp left, up the bank, and bear right on a footpath above the house to join the driveway. Follow the drive away from the house to reach a lane.

Turn right along the lane and soon pass under a bridge carrying the quarry road. Turn sharp right after the bridge, and go up the bank to reach a metal kissing gate signed for the coastal path on the left. Go through the kissing gate and bear half left up the sloping field. Bear left along the top edge of the field, go through a small gate in the corner, and bear left along the field edge to the lane.

3 Turn right up the lane and follow it as it climbs steeply. Where the lane turns sharp left, take the unsurfaced track ahead, signed for the Wales Coast Path again. This old lane continues the steep climb up towards **Bwlch yr Eifl**. Ignore paths off to the left and right, instead continuing ahead to reach a gate onto the open hillside.

The path continues to climb straight upwards with superb views back down to Trefor and across to Gyrn Ddu and Gyrn Goch. At the corner of a fence on the right, continue ahead again, more or less along the line of the overhead cables.

Just before the saddle, join a track leading down to the quarry. Bear left along the track to emerge at the high point of the pass where stunning views open out west along the coast.

© *Crown copyright and database rights 2014. Ordnance Survey. Licence number 100022856*

Pilgrim's road: *The spectacular view west from Bwlch Yr Eifl towards Nant Gwrtheryn, Nefyn and Carn Fadryn*

Detour: *A short walk to the summit of Yr Eifl*

The quarry workings make the summit on the right difficult to reach but the highest of Yr Eifl's triple tops on the left is straightforward to reach. A path leaves the track almost at the highest point on the saddle and makes the 200 metre climb in just under 1 kilometre. The path is visible all the way and curves round to the north just before summit. A path leaves the summit heading southwest to rejoin the coast path at the car park at Point 5.

The summit is a stunning spot, especially in clear conditions. The view east to the heights of Snowdonia takes in Bwlch Mawr, the shapely Nantlle Ridge, Moel Hebog and the Moelwynion. Across Cardigan Bay are the hills of southern Snowdonia — the Rhinogydd, Cadair Idris and beyond. To the west, the view takes in much of Llŷn as far as Pwllheli and Abersoch, as well as the hills of Carn Fadryn, Mynydd Rhiw and Mynydd Anelog in the far distance.

4 Continuing on the **official route**, beyond **Bwlch yr Eifl** the track descends gently above the dramatic fall into 👁 **Nant Gwrtheyrn** to reach a lane and parking area beside a conifer plantation.

Alternative route: *Bypassing the long descent into Nant Gwrtheryn*
Take the signed bridleway ahead. After a short walk across open ground pass under power lines and enter fields by a large gate. Go ahead keeping to the right-hand field edge and passing a line of large boulders. Go through the next gate and continue ahead until you reach a small gate in the wall on the right. Through the gate, continue in the same direction through the centre of the following field (with two farms

'Town of the Giants'

👁 **Tre'r Ceiri,** *the 'town of the giants', is one of Wales' most dramatic ancient monuments. Built around 100 BC and occupied well into the Roman period, it crowns the easternmost peak of Yr Eifl. Its stone ramparts survive in places to their original height, complete with parapet walks, access ramps and funnelled gateways. Within the walls are the remains of more than 150 stone hut circles. It's best reached by a path rising from the car park at Point 5.*

Distant views: *A vast westward panorama spreads out from the drystone ramparts of Tre'r Ceiri*

below to the left) to pass through a small gap in the remains of an earth covered stone wall.

Ahead there is a fine view along Llŷn's north coast past the sheltering arm of Trwyn Porth Dinllaen. It's backed by a line of knobbly hills that include Carn Fadryn and the distant Mynydd Anelog.

This section of footpath follows one of the old pilgrims' routes to Bardsey from Clynnog Fawr which came over Bwlch Yr Eifl and continued on to Nefyn. It was used during the Middle Ages when the holy island attracted pilgrims from all over Britain. (For more details, see pages 76-77.)

Drop to a gate in the lower corner of the field. Go through the gate and follow a low earthen bank ahead until you can turn right through a small gate in the wall. Go left alongside the wall to the corner, then turn right (ignoring the stile or gate ahead); then follow the wall down to a farm track and turn right. Take the left fork immediately and follow the track down towards the quarries on **Penrhyn Glas** to join the official route (see point 7).

5 For the **official route**, opposite the car park, turn right along the lane, which soon drops steeply through the trees into the valley. There are spectacular views into the valley from this road, especially from the first sharp bend.

Nant Gwrtheryn, or 'Vortigern's Valley'

'Vortigern's Valley'

A remote and atmospheric valley with a curious past

Nant Gwrtheryn or the 'Nant', as it is known locally, is a secluded valley bounded on three sides by the precipitous slopes of Yr Eifl but open to the sea on the fourth. Its name translates as 'Vortigern's Valley' and refers to the story of Vortigern, a 5th century Romano-British leader who sold out to the invading Saxons and fled to this hidden valley. Smollett's 18th century *Complete History of England* tells the traditional story. 'Vortigern, despised and neglected on all hands … fled for refuge to the almost inaccessible retreat at the foot of the mountain Rivel, where he spent the remainder of his days in terror and anxiety.'

A quarry was opened at Porth y Nant in the 1860s, with a jetty for steam ships to carry away the granite paving 'setts' to Liverpool, Birkenhead and Manchester. In the early days, most of the workers walked over the mountain every day from Trefor; later, workers' terraced houses, a manager's house and a Calvinist Methodist chapel were built in the valley. Porth y Nant was finally abandoned in the 1950s.

Today, the old Victorian village has been lovingly restored as a Welsh Language and Heritage Centre with conference and function rooms, accommodation and friendly café.

More information: Free admission. Open all year, 10.00am – 5.00pm, except Christmas and New Year. 01758 750334 | www.nantgwrtheyrn.org

Into the valley: *Dropping down towards Porth y Nant at the foot of Nant Gwrtheryn*

The road plunges steeply down the hillside through the trees to the **heritage centre** and **car park** at the bottom. Beyond the heritage centre and **café** (Caffi Meinir), the path slopes down to a viewpoint overlooking the beach. From here a constructed path snakes downhill to the shingly storm beach of **Porth y Nant**. Turn left and walk along the top of the beach past decaying winding gear to the ruined buildings above the shore ahead.

6 Leave the beach and climb up the slope to the ruins. A fingerpost on the grassy platform immediately in front of them indicates the continuation of the path to the right. This climbs diagonally and quite steeply at first, then swings right, more gently across the slope, crossing the occasional stream and weaving in and out of wind-stunted trees.

Keep an eye out for long-horned, brown and white goats among the scrub or on the slopes above. These wild animals, found across North Wales in places such as Snowdonia, the Rhinogydd and Yr Eifl, are thought to be British 'primitives' whose origins can be traced back to their introduction by Neolithic farmers.

Eventually a house comes into view above and ahead (**Cilau Isaf**) and the path leads up to a gate immediately in front of it.

7 Don't go through the gate; instead take the signed path to the right. Keep to the outside of fenced fields on the left, passing under overhead power lines. Cross the fence in the field corner and turn half-right down the field, passing under the cables once more. Pass the signed path to 'Porth-y-Nant' on the right, which leads down to the beach, and continue ahead to join a track. *(The alternative inland route rejoins the official coast path here.)* Turn right along the track, which is bordered on the right by large boulders. Shortly afterwards, bear left, following the signpost, and head up to the left of the quarries ahead.

8 At the top of the rise there is a bench and kissing gate on the left. Go through the kissing gate and walk ahead on a grassy track through the following fields. At the top of the gentle rise, the route ahead can be seen keeping to the left of walled fields. Go through the gate immediately ahead, cross the stream by **stepping stones** and bear right down along the lower field edge. Keep ahead and as 🦋 **St Beuno's Church** at **Pistyll** comes into view go through a kissing gate into the last field. A second kissing gate leads to a short track beside the **churchyard wall** to reach the lane.

Named after a 6th century hermit, 15th century St Beuno's Church at Pistyll was an important stopover on the medieval pilgrims' route to Bardsey. Pilgrims stayed at the nearby monastery or local inn, while the sick were treated in the Cae Hospice field or could rest in the smaller Cae Eisteddfod — or 'field of sitting or resting'. Since 1969 the church has been decorated every year with wild herbs and rushes laid on the floor at Christmas, Easter and the early August Lammas Festival.

9 From the churchyard turn right and follow the road over the bridge. At a fork in about 50 metres bear left through **castellated gate pillars**. *They're all that remain of the recently demolished Plas Pistyll Hotel, built originally by the Goddard family — owners of a famous 20th century silver polish company.*

Atmospheric St Beuno's Church at Pistyll

Pilgrims' view?: *Looking west towards the tip of Llŷn from the alternative route above Porth y Nant*

Walk along the drive towards a large house on the right and go through a kissing gate immediately in front of the house. Walk ahead through the field and the following small field to cross an access road by two kissing gates. Bear right down the field, with a small cottage on the right, then swing left across the bottom of a gorse covered bank (level with the cottage) on the left to a kissing gate. Go through the kissing gate (ignore a small gate on the left) and continue ahead along the top edge of the field to go through a kissing gate and cross a **small footbridge**. Keep ahead again beside the fence on the right and, at the outside corner, go ahead across the field a little to the left of centre. Bear left between **ruined stone farm buildings** and cross a stile on the right by a large gate. Bear right along the field edge beside a fence to reach the road by a kissing gate and small foot gate.

10 Turn left along the road. Within 50 metres, turn right down the driveway to 'Ty Mawr'. Just before the farmhouse, bear left up a ramp and go through a kissing gate. Follow the footpath ahead keeping the fence on your right. In 30 metres or so, the path bears away from the fence to take a contouring line above the farm. Cross a **stream** and go through a gate in the wall, then walk ahead to a marker post before bearing diagonally-right down to a gate in the far wall. This leads into the **garden of a house**. Walk ahead, passing in front of the house, and go through a kissing gate. The path continues ahead, soon passing below quarry spoil heaps.

11 Cross one of the **quarry inclines** by stone steps and continue ahead on the path that rises gently through the bracken. At a junction of paths, turn right to join an access road. Follow this ahead and at the T-junction turn left. Shortly the access road forks; keep left and follow the road past cottages. Immediately before the third cottage, take the enclosed footpath to the right of the driveway. Follow the path past the front of the cottage, then continue ahead passing '**Ffynnon John Morgan**' (a small spring on the left) to eventually join an access road. Turn left down the road and where this bends take the footpath ahead. This descends, overhung by hedges and then between fields, to emerge on the outskirts of **Nefyn**.

When the path ends, continue through playing fields, then turn right along a signed footpath between the churchyard wall of **St Mary's Church** and gardens on the right.

Old St Mary's, in Nefyn, was founded in the 6th century and during the Middle Ages was an important staging post for pilgrims on their way to Bardsey. The church was wholly rebuilt by the Victorians and once housed a local maritime museum. Notice the wrought iron sailing ship-shaped weathervane atop the tower.

At the road go ahead along '**Stryd y Mynach**' (Monks' Street). At the T-junction turn left and follow the road into the centre of **Nefyn** where this Day Section ends.

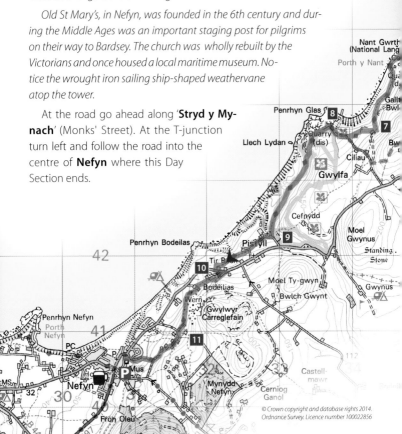

© Crown copyright and database rights 2014.
Ordnance Survey. Licence number 100022856

Nefyn to Porth Colmon

Distance: *12 miles/ 19.5 kilometres* | **Start:** *Nefyn (St Mary's Church) SH 309 407*
Finish: *Porth Colmon SH 194 343* | **Maps:** *OS Landranger 123 Llŷn Peninsula; and OS Explorer 254 Llŷn Peninsula East*

Outline: From Nefyn the route rounds the unusual promontory of Trwyn Porth Dinllaen before heading along grassy cliffs to Porth Colmon.

From the tiny seaside town of Nefyn, the clifftop path first heads past Morfa Nefyn and across the golf course to Porth Dinllaen with its sheltered bay, seal colony and pub on the beach. For the next 5 kilometres or so, the undulating path traces low, grassy cliffs above the rocky shore to the sandy beach at Porth Towyn. Beyond a series of sheltered fishing coves, the clifftop path arrives at Traeth Penllech's long sandy beach, at whose far end is the tiny picturesque harbour of Porth Colmon.

Services: *Café opposite Porth Dinllaen National Trust car park. Public toilets just off beach at Morfa Nefyn. Tŷ Coch Inn at Porth Dinllaen. Small summer café above Porth Towyn; detour to Tudweiliog pub, toilets and post office. Campsites above Towyn, Porth Ysgaden and Penrallt. No facilities at Porth Colmon; campsites up lane towards Llangwnnadl, plus seasonal shop. Nefyn Taxi Service 01758 720131*

👁 **Don't miss: Tŷ Coch Inn** — recently voted the '3rd best beach bar in the world' | **Porth Dinllaen** — 'the village on the beach', a sheltered harbour that once challenged Holyhead | **Porth Towyn** — popular sandy beach

▲ *Trwyn Porth Dinllaen*

Nefyn and Morfa Nefyn

Nefyn is a quiet, unspoiled seaside town with a useful range of shops, hotels, pubs, cafés, and other services. Old St Mary's Church in the heart of Nefyn dates from the 6th century and was an important stopping point on the medieval Pilgrims' Trail to Bardsey. By the 12th and 13th centuries, Nefyn was home to the Princes of Gwynedd, but it only really developed after it was granted official 'town' status by the Black Prince in 1355. It soon became an important trading centre famous for its shipbuilding and herring fleet. The town's coat of arms still features three herrings.

Nefyn and nearby Morfa Nefyn are fringed by two popular, long curving sandy beaches. They lead to the long arm of Trwyn Porth Dinllaen, with its Iron Age promontory fort, golf course, lifeboat station, seal colony and unmissable Tŷ Coch Inn — probably Wales' best pub on the beach. Once unsuccessfully promoted as the perfect embarkation port for Ireland, Porth Dinllaen is now managed and protected by the National Trust.

Porth Dinllaen and the distant Yr Eifl

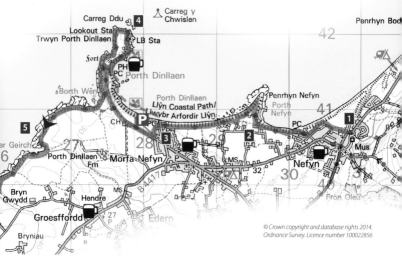

© Crown copyright and database rights 2014.
Ordnance Survey. Licence number 100022856

The route: **Nefyn to Porth Colmon**

1 From **Saint Mary's Church** in **Nefyn**, walk ahead to the end of the road and turn left into '**Stryd y Felin**'. Immediately after the road bends to the left, turn right onto a signed footpath between buildings. At a footpath T-junction, turn left and follow this footpath down to the coast.

From here you are treated to a fine view of the bay, from the tip of the headland of Trwyn Porth Dinllaen to the northern slopes of Yr Eifl which fall almost sheer to Caernarfon Bay. Although there are few ships in these coastal waters today, in the eighteenth and nineteenth centuries they were busy with sailing ships of all sizes. Over the centuries, countless ships have been lost on Llŷn's rocky northern shores.

The coast path left follows the edge of the slope above the beach for 100 metres or so before bearing left after a kissing gate. Follow a short path between gardens to an access road and turn right. Walk along the road with houses on either side to a T-junction and turn right. Don't follow the road down to the beach; instead, bear left almost immediately onto the coast path and follow this along the edge of the crumbling boulder clay cliffs high above the bay. There are grand views back along the coast to Yr Eifl and ahead to the tiny hamlet of **Porth Nefyn**.

2 At an access road directly above Porth Nefyn, turn right along the road briefly before bearing right where it bends left to a house. Follow the footpath through bracken to the end of the headland at **Penrhyn Nefyn**.

From here there is a grand view to the northeast of the stepped outlines of

Yr Eifl plunging into the sea from a height of over 1,800 feet. These hills provided a barrier to pilgrims en-route from Clynnog Fawr to Bardsey during the Middle Ages. Their route took them around the southern slopes of these hills, then down to the little church of Pistyll which sits in an exposed location on the very edge of the cliffs above Penrhyn Bodeilas. From here their route took them on to Nefyn, then along the north coast to Aberdaron. Some idea of just how arduous this journey was in those times is given by the fact that three pilgrimages to Bardsey were said to equal one to Jerusalem.

From **Penrhyn Nefyn** follow the footpath around the headland and continue on the cliff path above the next wide bay — **Porth Dinllaen**. At the time of writing a section of path has been closed due to collapse of the cliffs. Follow the footpath left as signed to an access driveway by a house. Turn right and at the lane turn right again. Where the lane turns left, go ahead down the driveway to a large house and just before the gateway pillars bear left onto an enclosed footpath that soon leads to the path again. Follow the coast path to a beach access road where there are public toilets.

The spectacular bay at Porth Dinllaen

Porth Dinllaen sunrise

The port that never was

Porth Dinllaen was once tipped to become the main ferry port for Ireland

For thousands of years, the Llŷn Peninsula was easily accessible only by sea and ships were the best way to travel or move goods. So the natural harbour formed by the sheltering arm of Trwyn Porth Dinllaen, near Nefyn, was both a welcome haven and an increasingly busy port. With more than a hundred acres of good anchorage, weak currents, no shoals or rocks, a firm clay bottom and up to 40 feet of water at low tide, the harbour soon became an important trading centre. Ships brought in empty barrels and salt for Nefyn's herring trade, and took away salted herring, cattle and pigs. Records show that more than 700 ships visited a year.

Then in 1803 local landowner and MP, William Madocks, decided to open up Llŷn to trade. He built new roads and an embankment across Traeth Mawr, established Porthmadog, and won parliamentary permission for a new hotel and pier at Porth Dinllaen. For a while it seemed the historic harbour might be chosen as the main ferry port for Ireland. His hopes were dashed in 1810 when Porth Dinllaen's bid was rejected by one vote in favour of Holyhead, on Anglesey. Today, the National Trust cares for this tiny, remote hamlet.

More information: www.llyn.info/info/walking/dinllaen.php. Pub on the beach: 01758 720498 | www.tycoch.co.uk

Beer on the beach: *The Tŷ Coch Inn at Porth Dinllaen was recently voted the third best beach bar in the world!*

Alternative Route: *Along the beach to Porth Dinllaen and the Tŷ Coch Inn.*

Rather than walk across the golf course, many people choose to walk along the broad sandy beach to 👁 **Porth Dinllaen**. Roughly half way along the coast, the path skirts behind a small group of houses hugging the low cliffs before continuing along the sand.

In summer, look out for a colony of sand martins nesting in holes in the sandy cliffs high above the beach.

3 For the **official route**, take the signed coast path directly opposite, and climb the steps to the National Trust car park and picnic area. Head away from the sea towards the car park entrance. Turn right and follow the road to the **Morfa Nefyn Golf Club** and the '**RNLI House**'. Go through the gate onto the golf course and follow the narrow tarmac road across the golf course and down to the tiny seaside hamlet of **Porth Dinllaen**.

Beyond the 👁 **Tŷ Coch Inn**, a narrow footpath passes between cottages before continuing around several tiny coves just above the high water mark.

At the **lifeboat station**, bear left up the concrete access road and, where this swings sharp left at the top of the rise, bear right onto a grassy, clifftop path.

Safe haven: *The long arm of grassy cliffs that curves around Porth Dinllaen forms a natural harbour that has been prized for centuries*

At low tide, the offshore rocks here are a favourite haul-out point for Atlantic grey seals, which bask lazily in the sun just above the surface of the sea.

4 Continue around the coast, which is now more exposed and rugged, before rising to a white-painted **'Coast Watch' lookout tower** at the tip of **Trwyn Porth Dinllaen**. Pass below and to the left of the lookout and follow the rough path back along the very edge of the golf course. The path runs along the western rim of the rocky peninsula, soon returning to the top of the narrow isthmus above Porth Dinllaen. Continue along the open, rugged coast as it curves to the right above **Borth Wen**.

5 At the end of the golf course, drop down to the tiny river and shingly bay at **Aber Geirch**.

Over a **wooden footbridge**, the coast path continues along the top of the cliffs above rock platforms, passing several inlets where rough tracks give coastal access to local boatmen. Ignore a signposted byway off to the left below 'Brynogolwyd' and continue along the coast path. Beyond a shallow stream valley running obliquely down to the sea, the path drops through a

wooden kissing gate above a long shingle strand, before rising through more kissing gates onto the high, sheep-cropped headland at **Penrhyn Cwmistir**.

6 Beyond another tiny inlet, the path runs on along the cliff top above low, lichen blackened rocks. Continue above the indented shore and cross another stream valley, to pass above a **natural rock arch**. From here, the path curves to the left to reach a long sweep of pebbly shore below 'Pant

Pub on the beach

The Tŷ Coch Inn at Porth Dinllaen has recently been voted the 'third best beach bar in the world'. Built in 1823 using red bricks brought in as ballast from Holland, the inn was soon nicknamed the 'red house' (or the Tŷ Coch) — a name that has stuck. At one time it was one of four pubs on the shore that served the busy local shipbuilding industry. Food served every day from 12-2.30pm. See www.tycoch.co.uk or call 01758 720498 for opening times.

Golden wonder: *Overlooking the ever-more popular sandy bay at Porth Towyn, near Tudweiliog*

Gwyn'. A little farther on, below 'Mynachdy', the path crosses a stream where a series of **small waterfalls** cascades into the sea.

The path winds on above several small **sandy bays** to arrive at another stream valley immediately above 👁 **Porth Towyn** — one of the largest and most popular sandy beaches on this exposed coast.

7 Turn left at a three way signpost, away from the coast, and then right, before the caravans, onto the coast path, which follows the top of the grassy slope above the beach.

Alternative route: *Along Porth Towyn beach*
Alternatively, turn right and follow the path down onto the sand. Turn left along the beach before climbing the grassy slopes at the far end of the bay to rejoin the coast path.

Detour: *To Tudweiliog village*
To reach **Tudweiliog**, turn left, away from the coast, and cross the lane to **Towyn Farm**. Once through the farmyard, bear left and follow the footpath across the fields. The village has a post office and general store, public toilets, caravan and campsite, and the friendly **Lion Hotel** with its popular food, large beer garden, real ale and accommodation.

To continue on the **official route** beyond **Towyn**, follow the coast path as it curves around the headland, before dropping down to a footbridge that spans a stream to a cluster of caravans above **Porth Ysglaig**. Ignore the rough vehicle access track that heads inland here; instead, take the grassy, uphill path to the right of the stream, which curves to the right above the pebbly beach. The path undulates above low, slumped cliffs to a tiny **picturesque cove** fringed by fishermen's huts, boats and rusty winches.

Climb to the painted tin shed on the prominent headland above the cove for panoramic views: east to Nefyn and the distinctive silhouette of Yr Eifl, and west down the coast to Mynydd Mawr.

8 Cross the cropped turf to a **ruined, stone gable end** and chimney above **Porth Ysgaden**. The path loops around the inlet's crumbling edge to a small parking area with benches and a concrete slip.

Protected by a long arm of rock, this sheltered inlet was once popular with local fishermen. Its name means 'port of herrings'. The substantial remains of storehouses and salting sheds can still be seen above the sandy cove.

Cross the access track and go through a wooden kissing gate onto the coast path, which runs over a broad grassy heath bordering the low cliffs. Dark clefts in the cliffs show the deep green sea below.

Just under a ½ mile/1 kilometre later, the path drops across a small stream to continue on the clifftop path

© Crown copyright and database rights 2014. Ordnance Survey. Licence number 100022856

Sea shed: *A fisherman's tin hut perches on the rocky headland above Porth Llydan*

above **Porth Gwylan** — a beautiful rocky cove protected by the National Trust. A path leads down to the shingle beach.

9 The coast path curves around the top of the cove. Ignore a signposted track towards a farm inland; instead continue along the coast towards 'Traeth Penllech 2m'.

The path continues across short turf above the rocky shore to reach '**Penrallt Coastal Campsite**' where a scallop shell and sign promise 'Pilgrims are welcome to camp or use our facilities'.

Within ½ mile/ 1 kilometre or so, the path curves around a headland and down to **Porth Ychain** — a small, pebbly cove fed by a stream. Walk along the top of the beach and climb the steps up the cliff at the far side. Above the beach, the path continues around lofty cliffs with open views over Caernarfon Bay.

Soon, the path skirts a grassy inlet in the cliffs with a cove at its foot, before crossing a stream that plummets through a rocky cleft into the sea below.

10 Beyond **Penrhyn Melyn**, the path sweeps above **Traeth Penllech**. At low tide this is a continuous stretch of sand; at high tide, a series of sandy

bays punctuated by rock stacks and outcrops. A grassy path snakes along the edge of the oblique cliffs, before dropping almost to the sand, crossing a stream and rising back to the clifftop.

Traeth Penllech is the largest sandy beach on Llŷn's rocky northern coast and is good for swimming. Largely off the beaten track, it's usually quiet, except in high summer. It was here that the ironclad barque 'Stewart' came to grief in 1901.

'King of the Sea'

The humble herring has sustained the ordinary people of northern Europe from time immemorial. Often called the 'King of the Sea', these steely backed, silver bellied fish moved in vast shoals around Britain's inshore waters. For centuries, Nefyn was known as the 'herring capital of Wales', and almost everyone on Llŷn depended on the annual herring catch. In glut years, local farmers carted away surplus fish to fertilise the fields. In poor years, everyone except the wealthy starved.

She was bound for New Zealand carrying a large consignment of whisky when disaster struck. The crew survived but it seems likely that some, at least, of the cargo found its way to local farms and cottages to enliven the long winter months.

Alternative route: *Along Traeth Penllech beach*

When the tide is low, it's a pleasant walk from here along the sand to the far end of the beach. There is a second chance to descend onto the beach a field or two later.

Continue along the beach towards the far end, but ignore the main exit path, which leads to a remote car park across the fields. Instead, continue either beyond a small headland to a stepped path up the grassy cliffs, or on to the far, rocky end of the beach, where a path leads up a concrete access ramp, through a gate beside a shed, and over clifftop fields to the pretty little fishing cove at **Porth Colmon**.

The **official route** runs along the top of the cliffs for the whole length of Traeth Penllech — with just one short detour down onto the beach about halfway along — to Porth Colmon where a lane comes down to the water's edge. The tiny, sheltered harbour of Porth Colmon is flanked by flat rocks called **Carreg y Defaid**, or 'sheep rocks', and backed by a rough turning circle, a stream and a few cottages.

The slipway is still used by local crab and lobster boats. Old tractors, lobster pots and marker buoys dot the grassy quay. Yet, even

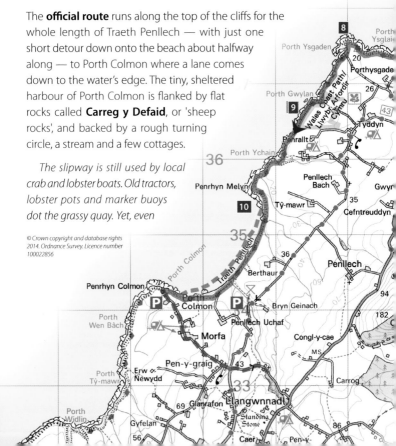

Big beach: *Traeth Penllech is the largest sandy beach on Llŷn's exposed northern coast*

within living memory, fishing was an important industry for almost everyone on Llŷn. Farming paused during the fishing season as people focussed instead on harvesting herring from the sea. The fish were sold fresh locally and, whenever the catch was large, salted and packed into barrels for transport to distant markets. Curing houses were a familiar sight at many of the tiny bays along this coast. By the end of the Victorian era, the herring shoals had moved away and by the late 1950s the industry ceased to exist.

Until the beginning of the nineteenth century, Porth Colmon was an important landing place for all kinds of goods for local people, from agricultural equipment to coal.

This Day Section ends at Porth Colmon. There are no amenities for walkers here; however, there are campsites and caravan parks less than ½ mile/1 kilometre way up the narrow lane towards **Llangwnnadl**, and a public phone box, church and summer shop a little farther on, in Llangwnnadl itself.

A 9-foot tall Bronze Age standing stone less than ½ mile south of St Gwynhoedl's Church at Llangwnnadl suggests the coast here was an important landfall in prehistoric times. Around the church are small, elongated and slightly curved fields: which are probably surviving medieval field strips, or 'quillets'.

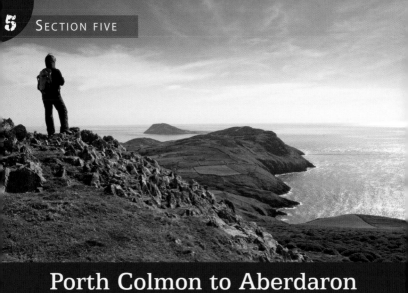

Porth Colmon to Aberdaron

Distance: *14 miles/ 22 kilometres* | **Start:** *Porth Colmon SH 194 343*
Finish: *Aberdaron SH 173 265* | **Maps:** *OS Landranger 123 Llŷn Peninsula; and OS Explorer 253 Llŷn Peninsula West*

Outline: This semi-wild section around the tip of Llŷn seems to encapsulate everything that makes the 'Land's End of Wales' so special.

From Porth Colmon, the path follows the cliffs above countless tiny bays to the popular sandy beach at Porthor, or 'Whistling Sands'. From here the path rises steadily along the National Trust protected coast past Mynydd Carreg and Mynydd Anelog to Mynydd Mawr, with its panoramic views to Bardsey Island. Inland are the tiny ancient fields of Uchmynydd, a stronghold of Welsh language and culture. Beyond the headlands of Braich y Pwll and Pen y Cil, the path follows the clifftop past Porth Meudwy — the embarkation point for Bardsey, to the compact village of Aberdaron.

Services: *Sparse on this section. Seasonal beach café (Apr - Oct) at Porthor/ Whistling Sands. Toilets in NT car park. Aberdaron has a National Trust visitor centre, two pubs/ hotels, general store, bakery, Spar shop, fish & chip shop, and several cafés. Campsites inland below Mynydd Mawr, near Porth Meudwy and near Aberdaron. Bardsey boats from Porth Meudwy — book ahead only. Abersoch Taxi Service 07990 630748*

Don't miss: Llangwnnadl Church – Saint Gwynhoedl's shrine and pilgrim's church | **Whistling Sands** – the famous 'squeaking' sands at Porthor | **Bardsey, or 'Ynys Enlli'** – views across the Sound to this timeless holy island

▲ *Mynydd Mawr and Bardsey from Mynydd Anelog*

Llangwnnadl

Today Llangwnnadl is a tiny, straggling but ancient settlement with caravan and camping sites and a seasonal shop, just up the lane from Porth Colmon.

But back in the Middle Ages, Llangwnnadl Church was one of the most important stopping places on the Pilgrims' Route to Bardsey. In fact, the 'Shrine of Gwynhoedl' became so popular that the church had to be enlarged with a new south aisle and arcade to accommodate all its supplicants. In evidence, the field next to the church is still called Cae Eisteddfa, or the 'place to sit and rest'.

Until the early 19th century, when road and rail links to Llŷn improved, most goods arrived by sea, and Porth Colmon was an important landing place for this part of the peninsula, for everything from coal to farm goods. Today, fresh crab and lobster can sometimes be bought at Porth Colmon in season.

Ancient St Gwynhoedl's Church, at Llangwnnadl

The route: **Porth Colmon to Aberdaron**

Detour: *To the church of Saint Gwynhoedl*

Before leaving Porth Colmon, it's worth making a short detour inland to visit the atmospheric, medieval pilgrims' 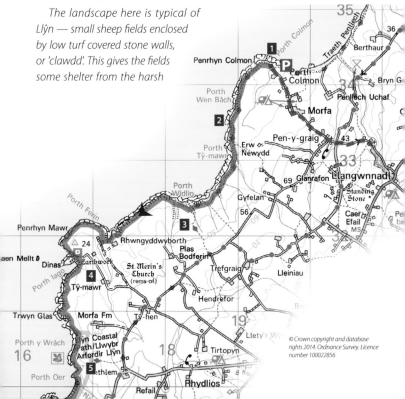 church of St Gwynhoedl at **Llangwnnadl**.

1 From the tiny harbour at **Porth Colmon**, the coast path continues over a signposted wooden footbridge across a stream. On the far side, a flight of shallow stone steps heads up the low cliffs onto **Penrhyn Colmon**.

As you leave Porth Colmon look back for a fine view of the bay backed by the shapely tops of Yr Eifl and Carn Fadryn. Farther along the coast path, views open out to the south and west to include Mynydd Rhiw and Mynydd Anelog at the southern end of the peninsula.

From here the coast path skirts the top of grassy cliffs above low rock platforms fringing the sea below. Go through a waymarked kissing gate and continue along the clifftop.

The landscape here is typical of Llŷn — small sheep fields enclosed by low turf covered stone walls, or 'clawdd'. This gives the fields some shelter from the harsh

© Crown copyright and database rights 2014. Ordnance Survey. Licence number 100022856

Once busy: *Porth Colmon was once busy with local boats carrying farm goods and animals*

winds that blow in from the Irish Sea. Trees are scarce except for a few stunted hawthorns that lean dramatically inland, giving some idea of the winter gales that batter this open coast.

In early summer the 'unimproved' grassy margins here are bright with wildflowers; look out for yarrow, yellow vetch, knapweed, clover, rockrose, hawks-bit, wild thyme and ladies bedstraw. These in turn support a wealth of butterflies: meadow browns, gatekeepers, small white and the occasional small copper.

2 Beyond **Ffos Nant**, **Trwyn Cam** and **Porth Wen Bach**, the path goes through a waymarked kissing gate and kinks sharply to the left above the pebbly cove of **Porth Tŷ-llwyd**. A few hundred metres later, the path reaches a deep stream valley marked by a double signpost that points back to 'Porth Colman ¾' and onwards to 'Porth Widlin ¾'. Beyond the wooden footbridge the path rises to continue along the grassy cliff top. *On the headland nearby is a white stone inscribed in Welsh in memory of 'John Hughes Griffiths'.*

The path curves gently to the right above a long rocky bay before crossing another wooden footbridge where a clear stream runs through small pools before plunging over the cliff in a small **waterfall**.

3 Beyond two further shallow stream valleys, the path bends to the right around a sheep-grazed headland at the far end of **Porth Tŷ Mawr**. .

Poet's choice?: *Remote and lovely, Porth Iago was a favourite of RS Thomas, the renowned Welsh poet and one-time vicar of Aberdaron*

After a footbridge above **Porth Widlin**, the path bears right, up the bank, to run beside fenced fields on the left. At another stream valley, the path turns right and drops to go through a kissing gate and over a footbridge. Rising steeply up the bank, the path continues over the lower half of the coastal slope, well below the fenced fields above.

Beyond a gate and kissing gate the path reaches **Porth Ferin**, a two-pronged inlet, whose stony coves are backed by a farm and cottages. At the first inlet turn right briefly onto a track running down to the sea, before bearing left up the bank to continue beside fenced fields. The path skirts the next larger inlet where there is a shingle beach; it then crosses more open ground, but still with fenced fields on the left, in the approach to the next inlet and beach — **Porth Iago**. Winter storms over recent years have taken their toll on this once beautiful cove, removing much of its silver sand. In the right conditions however, it is still a lovely place to be.

4 The signposted coast path runs above the beach, still tight against the fenced fields to the left. Beyond the next headland — **Trwyn Glas**, the 'green headland', is **Porth y Wrâch**, or 'port of the witch'.

5 The fine looking stretch of sand ahead is **Porthor**, or '**Whistling Sands**'. The path crosses open ground marked by white-topped posts, then continues through a metal kissing gate with tiny coves down to the right. (Ignore the old kissing gate on the left, which runs up a marshy valley and green lane to the road). Within 100 metres, the official route branches off to the left through a wooden kissing gate to skirt along the top of the cliffs above Porthor.

Graded grains

The popular National Trust beach at 👁 **Porthor** *is also known by locals as* **'Whistling Sands'**. *The intriguing name refers to the squeaking sound the sand makes underfoot. It's one of only two beaches in Europe where this phenomenon occurs and is caused by the unusual shape of the grains of sand. Surfers love the beach, too, especially when there's a south-easterly wind with a south-westerly swell at high tide.*

Alternative route: *Along Porthor/ 'Whistling Sands' beach*

To walk along 👁 **Porthor/ 'Whistling Sands'**, bear right here and descend to a gap in a stone wall before dropping down steps to the sand. There's a seasonal (Easter-October) beach café, shop and access road at the far end of beach. The onward path around the headland at the far end is now closed due to a landslip. To rejoin the official route from the end of the beach, head left up the access road and turn right into the National Trust car park at the top.

6 The **official route** follows the top of the cliffs around the bay, before curving away from the coast to arrive opposite the **National Trust car park** at the top of the beach access road.

Cross the road into the car park and in about 200 metres, turn right by the **toilets** on the signed path. This runs through low trees to a headland above the south-western end of the beach.

Follow the path along the cliffs for about 1 mile/ 1.5 kilometres, passing the two islets of **Dinas Bach** and **Dinas Fawr** — the 'little stronghold' and the 'big stronghold'.

There are small sandy coves around these islands, which can be reached easily at low tide and make fine picnic spots.

7 Just beyond Dinas Fawr there is an inlet and a small but distinct valley running inland — this is **Porthorion**. The waymarked path veers leftwards here and a link path leads inland to the road. The coast path turns sharp right at a marker post immediately before a simple plank bridge to cross the stream by a wooden footbridge. Rise directly up the slope from the footbridge.

The Wales Coast Path continues beyond the popular sandy beach at Porthor

Still waters: *The deep inlet at Porthorion is part of a section of coast protected by the National Trust*

The path continues along the outside edge of fields to your left until the way ahead is fenced. The path swings left here through a gate in the corner and continues ahead on the rising path. Climb steadily through an open area of rough grazing dotted with gorse and heather, with a small farm away to the left. Go through a wooden footgate in the wall/fence and continue straight ahead on the clear, gently rising path, until you reach a track over a rise, in about 350 metres, with a small cottage down the hillside to the left.

8 Bear right and follow the grassy track as it curves uphill keeping right when the track forks. At the top of the rise, there is a glorious view ahead along the cliffs to Mynydd Mawr, with Bardsey peeping over its shoulder. Nearer at hand you will see a small **white cottage** with a wall-enclosed field immediately in front on the slopes of **Mynydd Anelog**. Follow the track to the cottage.

Keep to the right of the cottage, beside the walled field, then take the contouring path ahead as it curves around the hillside.

Shortly you get views out towards **Mynydd Mawr** again and a small gate is visible below. The path zig-zags down beside the wall and goes through the gate in the corner. The path now heads down between gorse and bracken aiming for the right-hand side of a field below. At the lower outside corner of the field turn left with the field boundary and follow the path above the deep, rocky inlet of **Porth Llanllawen**.

Coastal hills: *Following the coast path over Mynydd Anelog with Mynydd Mawr ahead*

9 Half a kilometre farther on the path descends gently to cross a footbridge over the stream by the National Trust sign above **Porth Llanllawen**. Ascend steeply beyond the stream and continue along the coastal slope. Go through a kissing gate in the top left-hand corner of the slope and walk ahead up a small field and through a second kissing gate. This leads onto the open hillside of **Mynydd Mawr**. Take the rising path directly ahead marked by white-topped posts carrying the Wales Coast Path waymarkers.

After winding across often steep, heathery hillsides, the path eventually joins the concrete road near the **summit of Mynydd Mawr**. Turn right and you will soon be on the summit with its superb views of the surrounding coast. It's a good place for a break.

The summit offers extensive views along the coast to the south and inland to the hills of Mynydd Anelog, Carn Fadryn and Mynydd Rhiw. Nearer at hand lie the ancient walled fields of Uwchmynydd. Yet it's the island of 👁 **Bardsey**, *or* **'Ynys Enlli'**, *two miles across the Sound to the west, that demands attention.*

10 From the **old coastguard lookout**, follow the concrete footpath ahead down the front of the hillside with Bardsey directly ahead. Lower down there is a concrete platform. Keep ahead, still descending until you reach a signed contouring footpath (white-topped Wales Coast Path posts). Turn left and

Looking across the Sound to Bardsey

'Island in the tide'

Bardsey is the fabled 'island of 20,000 saints'

Lying two miles across the Sound at the remote, western tip of Llŷn, Bardsey Island, or *Ynys Enlli* — the 'island in the tide' — has fascinated people since time immemorial. Although Bardsey has been a place of pilgrimage since the early years of Christianity, hut circles and other evidence confirm people have lived here since at least Neolithic times.

The island later became a focus for the early Celtic Christians and St Cadfan is said to have built the first monastery here in the sixth century. Medieval bards called Bardsey *'the land of indulgences, absolution and pardons, the road to Heaven and the gate to Paradise'.* In fact, so holy was the island that a twelfth century Pope declared three pilgrimages to Bardsey equalled one to Jerusalem. The monastery later became an Augustinian abbey until Henry VIII's Dissolution of the monasteries in 1537. Now only the roofless abbey tower survives, where a Celtic cross commemorates the 20,000 saints said to be buried in the shallow soil.

Today the island is recognised as both nationally and internationally important for wildlife, and protected by the Bardsey Trust and Natural Resources Wales.

More information: For more about day trips and staying on Bardsey, see: **www.bardsey.org**

Journey's end?: *Bardsey Island, the mystical goal of countless pilgrims over the centuries*

follow the path with spectacular views down to the sea and across the sound to Bardsey. Shortly the path swings right-wards around a broad grassy terrace marked by the familiar white-topped waymarker posts.

A hairy scramble down the cliffs below takes you to the ancient **St. Mary's Well**. *Despite being washed by the waves, the water in the natural rock basin is virtually fresh. It's said pilgrims would wash their feet here as a blessing before crossing the treacherous Sound to Bardsey.*

11 The path contours to cross a stream before swinging right on a diagonal rise. Continue round to the next inlet, the deep, rocky **Porth Felen**, where seals can often be seen basking on the rocks. Go through a gate in the wall/fence directly above the inlet and follow the path ahead along the top of the cliffs to a second gate. Through the gate, the path continues ahead close to fenced fields on the left. Go through another gate in the crossing wall and keep ahead again, this time through more open ground, following the white-tipped waymarkers.

12 Continue until you reach a point almost level with a small, rocky islet out to the right called **Carreg Ddu**, or the 'black rock'. The path swings left now up over steeper, rough ground with the deep cliff-lined inlet of **Parwyd**

to the right. Where you meet the fence, turn left and follow it to a kissing gate in the corner by a **National Trust stone pillar** ('Bychestyn') and information board in the upper field corner. Turn right through the kissing gate and follow the field edge ahead to a gate in the far corner. Go through the gate and walk ahead again to a kissing gate on the right that leads onto the headland of **Pen y Cil** — Uwchmynydd's southern-most point, protected by the National Trust.

'Port of the Hermits'

The sheltered cove of Porth Meudwy, near Aberdaron, was the traditional embarkation point for pilgrims crossing to Bardsey, or Ynys Enlli. During bad weather the island can be cut off for weeks, and pilgrims often had to wait patiently in Aberdaron. Today, modern fast boats still leave Porth Meudwy for Bardsey. For details, see: www.bardseyboattrips.com.

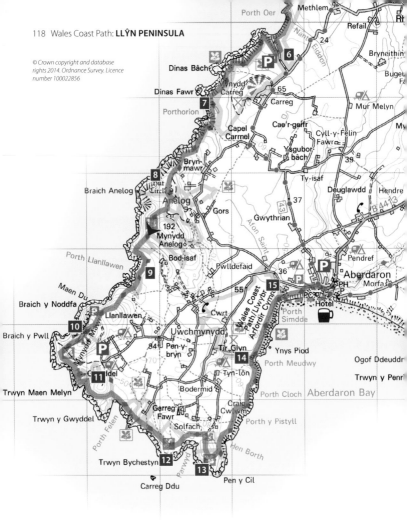

There is a fine view from this southwestern tip of Llŷn taking in the wide sweep
of Aberdaron Bay with its two islands — Gwylan Fawr and Gwylan Fach (or, literally, 'Large Gull Island' and 'Little Gull Island') and the headland at Penarfynydd,
one of the enclosing arms of the infamous Hell's Mouth. Look westwards for your
last glimpse of Bardsey and the treacherous waters of Bardsey Sound.

13 Follow the path ahead past the **cairn** and continue down beside the
fence on the left. Lower down the path swings left, passes through a kissing
gate and continues ahead with a small walled field on the right. Beyond a
second kissing gate the coast path keeps to the outer edge of fields on the

Aberdaron Bay: *Heading into Aberdaron Bay from Pen y Cil*

left on the very edge of the steep coastal slope. Down to the right are **Hen Borth** (the 'old harbour'), **Porth y Pistyll** ('harbour of the waterfall') and **Porth Cloch** ('harbour of the bell'). Continue to **Porth Meudwy** — a sheltered inlet where the path drops down steps.

The tiny cove of Porth Meudwy, whose name means the 'harbour of the hermit', is the closest safe embarkation point for Bardsey. Medieval pilgrims waited in Aberdaron until the weather cleared before walking along the cliff path to catch the boat here.

14 From Porth Meudwy climb the steps ahead and continue on the coast path towards Aberdaron.

15 As you approach Aberdaron, steps lead down to another small inlet, called **Porth Simdde**, at the western end of the beach. If the tide is out the walk along the beach makes a fine, leisurely end to this Day Section; although you will have to ford the shallow **Afon Daron** where it spreads out across the sand.

Otherwise, the **official route** bears left on a footbridge across the tiny **Afon Saint**, then climbs stone steps to the clifftop. Head right on an enclosed path high above the beach. When it ends at a metal kissing gate, turn right, downhill on the road into the centre of **Aberdaron** and the end of this Day Section.

Aberdaron to Hell's Mouth

Distance: *11 miles/ 18 kilometres* | **Start:** *Centre of Aberdaron SH 173 265*
Finish: *Car park at the southern end of Hell's Mouth beach, at Pentowyn SH 284 267*
Maps: *OS Landranger 123 Llŷn Peninsula; and OS Explorer 253 Llŷn Peninsula West*

Outline: Another semi-wild Day Section full of variety, spectacular views, ancient monuments and wildlife.

From the compact village of Aberdaron, the path runs along a stream valley and over fields to the coast at tiny Porth Ysgo, before traversing the rocky, heather-clad slopes of Mynydd Penarfynydd and Graig Fawr, with broad sea views. Beyond the National Trust manor house and gardens at Plas yn Rhiw, the path drops to the four-mile long sands of Porth Neigwl, or 'Hell's Mouth'. From the main car park at the far end of the beach, it's a short detour to the pub and pilgrims's church in nearby Llanengan.

Services: *There are few services beyond Aberdaron. Snacks, drinks and ice creams from the National Trust ticket office at Plas yn Rhiw. Campsites above western end of Hell's Mouth and inland from the car park at Pentowyn Dunes. Seasonal tea and burger van often here too. Emergency phone in car park. Friendly pub (Sun Inn) with beer garden and restaurant in Llanengan. Abersoch Taxi Service 07990 630748*

Don't miss: St Hywyn's Church – the penultimate stop on the medieval Pilgrim's Trail | **Plas yn Rhiw** – a quirky National Trust manor house | **Hell's Mouth** – Llŷn's famous four-mile surf beach

▲ *Looking back to Bardsey from Mynydd Penarfynydd*

Aberdaron

Aberdaron is a tiny, picturesque whitewashed village in a small valley close to the tip of Llŷn, centred around two ancient bridges that span the confluence of Afon Daron and Afon Cyll-y-felin. For centuries, it has been the traditional jumping off point for pilgrims awaiting safe passage to Bardsey. Today, modern pilgrims, bird watchers and walkers can still catch the boat across the Sound to Bardsey from nearby Porth Meudwy.

Known as the 'Cathedral of Llŷn', Aberdaron's historic 👁 **Church of St Hywyn** and its dramatic graveyard dominate the slopes above the village. After years of coastal erosion, they are now protected by modern sea defences. Dating back to 1137, but built on an earlier 6th-century religious site, the church contains early Christian relics and an exhibition commemorating RS Thomas, the renowned Welsh poet and one-time vicar of Aberdaron.

Look out, too, for the new National Trust Visitor Centre at the heart of Aberdaron with its fascinating displays, visitor information, events programme and small local shops.

Aberdaron clusters around the mouth of Afon Daron, close to the 'Land's End' of Llŷn

The route: **Aberdaron to Hell's Mouth**

1 From the old stone bridge over **Afon Daron** in the centre of **Aberdaron**, the coast path heads uphill, away from the sea, past the Post Office and thatched bakers' shop and cafe, on the narrow B4413. It's signposted to 'Pwllheli'. Less than 100 metres later, look for a Wales Coast Path fingerpost on the right. The path initially runs alongside a wall, above caravans, then heads inland along the left-hand side of the narrow valley of **Afon Daron**.

In around ½ mile/1 kilometre look for a well-made footbridge on the right, cross the river and follow the good path ahead rising out of the valley to go through two kissing gates. Take the short field path on the right to reach the road beside **'Morfa' farm**.

2 Cross the road and walk down the track opposite ('**Morfa Mawr Caravan & Campsite**'). In around 100 metres go through the kissing gate on the left into a large field and follow the right of way along the right-hand edge. In the bottom corner go ahead into the next small field to a kissing gate at a junction of fences. Through the gate, turn right immediately through a second kissing gate and follow a fenced footpath down to the edge of the cliffs overlooking **Aberdaron Bay**.

Head left along the grassy cliff-top path. This is fenced initially, then runs along the upper edge of the open coastal slope. As you approach the headland of **Trwyn y Penrhyn**, the coast path keeps beside the wall/fence as it turns left. The path is straightforward now with fields to the left and impressive views ahead.

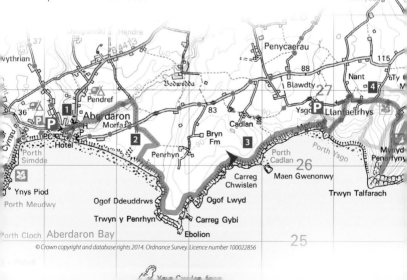

© Crown copyright and database rights 2014. Ordnance Survey. Licence number 100022856

Last prayers: *Twelfth century St Hywyn's Church at Aberdaron was the final stopping place for medieval pilgrims en-route to Bardsey*

3 The rocky islet of **Maen Gwenonwy** has been visible for much of this section. When you are directly above it, go through a kissing gate and bear left to follow a section of path enclosed by fences high above **Porth Cadlan**.

At the end of the fenced section the path turns left, briefly away from the coast, over a simple plank bridge and through a kissing gate into a large field. Contour around the field following white-topped waymarker posts. Through a kissing gate, the path continues across steeply sloping pastures high above the sea, with **Porth Ysgo** visible ahead.

The path soon drops to a waymarked wooden footbridge above a deep stream valley. Roughly ½ kilometre later, the path descends to a second broader stream valley that plunges over a **waterfall** into Porth Ysgo. Cross the stream on an ancient footbridge formed of huge stone slabs.

Detour: *To visit Porth Ysgo beach*

Bear right after the footbridge to reach the cliff edge where a timber staircase zig-zags down the cliff to the shore.

Porth Ysgo was a favourite spot of RS Thomas, the renowned Welsh poet and vicar of Aberdaron. There is a high waterfall at the western end of the cove, which is also popular with sea anglers. Ruined manganese mines and the surrounding cliff scenery give this section of coast a Cornish feel.

Islands in the tide: *From the National Trust owned headland of Penarfynydd, the panorama takes in the tiny offhshore islands of Ynys Gwlan-fawr and Ynys Gwlan-bach, with Bardsey beyond*

The **official route** continues on a section of raised path and soon meets a broad grassy path that once led down to the beach at a T-junction. Turn left here, away from the coast through a kissing gate, and head up the broad stream valley of **Nant y Gadwen** to a lane junction.

> Detour: *To visit the little church of St Maelrhys in nearby Llanfaelrhys*
> Turn left along the lane from the junction. *The simple, single chambered stone building contains a medieval nave and font and later chancel. The poet RS Thomas' first wife, artist Elsi Eldridge, is buried in the churchyard.*

4 From the junction, follow the signed coast path sharp right along the lane, past **Llawenan Farm**. Ignore the footpath sign that points across the fields close to the junction. Less than 200 metres beyond the farm, look for a Wales Coast Path fingerpost pointing across the fields to the right. Head across two fields, keeping to the lefthand side, to a lane immediately below **Penarfynydd Farm**, sheltered below the long ridge of **Mynydd Penarfynydd**.

Cross the farm access lane and walk through the farmyard to a waymarked gate to the left of the farmhouse. Go through the gate and turn right beside the wall. Shortly, where the wall begins to descend, the path bears left cut-

ting gently up the open hillside. Continue to the end of the headland high above **Trwyn Talfarach** for superb views along the coast to Bardsey island. *In addition to the views, the heather and gorse clad slopes are a good place to watch for Llŷn's iconic breeding choughs, which often tumble over the headland in noisy, acrobatic flight. This is a good area for peregrines, too.*

5 Retrace your steps for a about 150 metres and bear right (waymarker post) on a narrow path which rises to the triangulation pillar on **Penarfynydd**.

Choughs on Llŷn

Around five percent of Britain's choughs are found on Llŷn. Choughs are rare but distinctive members of the crow family with curved red bills and red legs. They breed on mountains and sea cliffs in western Britain, where they probe with their curved bills for insects in the cropped mountain turf. Watch and listen for their bounding flight, finger-like wing tip feathers, and ringing 'kee-aar' call. You are most likely to see them around the rocky tip of Llŷn.

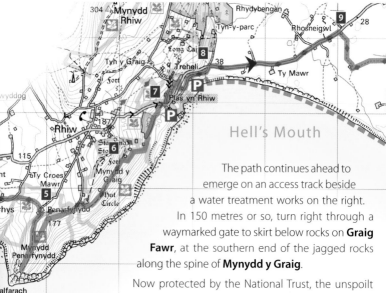

Hell's Mouth

The path continues ahead to emerge on an access track beside a water treatment works on the right. In 150 metres or so, turn right through a waymarked gate to skirt below rocks on **Graig Fawr**, at the southern end of the jagged rocks along the spine of **Mynydd y Graig**.

Now protected by the National Trust, the unspoilt open common land on **Mynydd y Graig** is still grazed by local sheep. *In late summer, the seaward slopes are bright with purple heather and yellow, wind-trimmed western gorse punctuated with tall foxgloves and pale, wiry grasses. Heated by the sun, the honey-and-wood scent of heather fills the air. Brown hares love these open slopes, too.*

In summer, stonechats click from gorse patches and kestrels sweep and hover over the heath. Parties of up to twenty or so choughs often twist over the cliffs. There are stunning views, too, out to sea and eastwards over the vast bay of Porth Neigwl, or Hell's Mouth, backed by the long tongue of Mynydd Cilan.

The broad grassy path swings left to undulate across the hillside slopes for almost ½ mile/1 kilometre.

6 Pass a small wall-enclosed field and as you approach a second field, a little further on with a tiny stone cottage ahead, bear right at a fork. The path keeps to the right-hand side of the field beside the wall with wide views ahead to the distant hills of Snowdonia. Keep to the right of another small walled field before turning right, to head steeply down beside the wall. Lower down turn left to follow the path beside the overgrown wall. In around 100 metres the path enters a small wood keeping to the lower edge of the trees to enter fields through a gated footbridge. The path heads up a sloping field to reach a quiet lane.

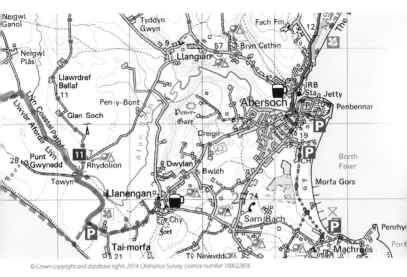

© Crown copyright and database rights 2014. Ordnance Survey. Licence number 100022856

7 Turn right, then left almost immediately into the driveway to the National Trust's 16th century manor house of 👁 **Plas yn Rhiw**. Walk up the driveway past the house on the left and turn right as signed to pass through the car park and past the **ticket office and shop** (local guidebooks, ice creams and cold drinks). A well-made footpath continues ahead into the woods. In around 30 metres, turn right down steps to zig-zag down to the lane. Bear right across the road taking the path opposite. This leads down to the old lane, closed a few years ago due to landslip. Turn left and walk along the lane.

Keep right at a fork immediately after **Treheli** farm. The tarmacked lane runs past **Treheli Farm campsite** perched above the western end of Hell's Mouth.

The **official route** turns inland here to avoid the 4 mile/6.5 kilometre hike along Hell's Mouth beach. The constantly eroding clay cliffs are prone to slump and collapse and high tides can cover the beach entirely.

Alternative route: *Along Hell's Mouth beach*
Generations of walkers have delighted in heading along 👁 **Hell's Mouth beach**. Armed with common sense and tide tables, and avoiding bad weather, it should be perfectly safe. **However, recent winter storms have inflicted considerable damage to the unstable clay cliffs making access to the beach more difficult.** Keep well away from the base of the cliffs, which change to open sand dunes roughly half way along. The choice (and the responsibility) is entirely yours.

Four-mile beach: *A surfers' paradise, Porth Neigwl, or 'Hell's Mouth', is the Llŷn's longest beach*

To reach the beach, turn right through a signposted metal kissing gate just before the lane rejoins the road. Across the grass, a well used but constantly slipping path descends through scrub over gentle clay cliffs to the beach; the last section of the path is often eroded by winter storms and may entail a brief scramble onto the sand. Once on the beach, turn left and head south-east for the dunes and car park at the distant far end.

The first half of **Hell's Mouth** is often deserted but the eastern end of the beach, closer to the car park at Pentowyn, is a favourite with holidaymakers and surfers from nearby Abersoch. After 2 miles/ 3.5 kilometres or so, it's possible to ascend from the beach and walk through the dunes parallel with the shore. Look out for the exit path to the car park in about 2½ miles/ 4 kilometres through **Pentowyn Dunes**, south of Llanengan.

8 Otherwise, for the **official inland route**, ignore the path down to Hell's Mouth on the right; instead, walk ahead to the T-junction and turn right along the road. Follow the road for around 1¼ miles/ 2 kilometres.

9 Immediately before a stone house on the right, called '**Neigwl Newydd'**, a Wales Coast Path signpost points to a kissing gate into the fields on the right. Go through the gate, walk ahead through the fields. In the third field, bear half-right in the direction of a distant **ruined cottage**.

Through a gate and footbridge, walk ahead past the ruin and where you cross the old field boundary (the earth covered '*clawdd*'), turn left through

Ship's graveyard

Porth Neigwl, better known as 'Hell's Mouth', was notorious for shipwrecks in the age of sail. Enclosed by the two rocky headlands of Mynydd Cilan and Mynydd Penarfynydd, the bay's wide mouth and southwest orientation made it the perfect trap for sailing ships. Caught by the prevailing winds, ships were blown into the bay, quickly passing the point of no return — and were irrevocably doomed.

the large open field. As you approach the fence ahead, you will see a small footgate beside the larger field gate. Head for this, go through the gate and continue through the following field to pass through another footgate. Keep ahead in the next field, aiming for the outside corner of the field marked by an **upright stone pillar**. Pass the pillar, keeping ahead beside the fence on the left, to reach a large gate in the corner and a farm track. Don't follow the track ahead; instead, turn sharp right and walk back diagonally across the field to reach a small footgate in the fence on the left.

10 Go through the gate, cross a farm track and walk ahead beside the fence on the left, with farm buildings in the distance ahead. Go through a bridle gate in the fence on the left and walk ahead across the field to a second bridle gate. Go through the gate and turn right, around the field edge. In the far corner, two foot gates and a sleeper bridge on the right lead onto a farm track with a **ruined brick building** ahead. Turn left along the track for a few metres, then go right along the field edge (and past the brick building) where the track turns sharp left. (There's a campsite just up the lane to the left).

As you pass into the next field, you'll see a narrow river — **Afon Sôch** — on the left. The next stretch keeps more or less beside the river and takes a direct line through the following fields to reach a quiet lane at **Pont Towyn** bridge, next to **Towyn Farm**.

The four-mile long beach of Porth Neigwl, or 'Hell's Mouth'

Pilgrims' church: *The parish church of St Einion at Llanengan is one of the oldest in Llŷn*

11 Turn right along the lane. Follow the lane to the beach car park (Hell's Mouth) where this Day Section ends.

(If you're taking the alternative route along **Hell's Mouth** beach, turn left up the beach path to the reach the car park at **Pentowyn**.)

Detour: *To Llanengan church and pub*

For **Llanengan** with its pilgrims' church and popular **Sun Inn**, turn left along the lane for about 1mile/1.5 kilometres.

Beautiful medieval St Einion's Church overlooks Porth Neigwl (or Hell's Mouth) from the heart of the village of Llanengan. Almost within sight of Bardsey, the church was an important stopping place on southern pilgrims' route to the 'holy island'. Look for the outline of an Iron Age hillfort and a later mine chimney on the hill behind the village.

Hell's Mouth to Llanbedrog

Distance: *14 miles/ 22 kilometres* | **Start:** *Car park at the southern end of Hell's Mouth beach at Pentowyn SH 284 267* | **Finish:** *Llanbedrog SH 330 316* | **Maps:** *OS Landranger 123 Llŷn Peninsula; and OS Explorer 253 Llŷn Peninsula West*

Outline: Beyond Mynydd Cilan's heathery headland, the path visits the upmarket surf village of Abersoch before following the beach to Llanbedrog.

After a short climb from Hell's Mouth onto Mynydd Cilan, the clifftop Path crosses open heathland to pass above sandy Porth Ceiriad bay. With striking views to St Tudwal's islands, the path drops to the lively surfer's village of Abersoch. The path then follows the long sandy beach past the Warren to climb over lofty Mynydd Tir-y-cwmwd headland with its 'Tin Man' scupture, before descending sharply to pretty Llanbedrog.

Services: *Abersoch offers everything from banks, a post office, pharmacy, small supermarket and lots of pubs and bars, to surf and outdoor shops, a chandlery, restaurants, cafés and takeaways. Llanbedrog has a beach bistro, art gallery, shop and café at Plas Glyn y Weddw, plus a pub, post office, pharmacy, public toilets, and several nearby campsites. Abersoch TIC 01758 712929. Abersoch Taxi Service 07990 630748.*

Don't miss: Mynydd Cilan – beautiful, heathery clifftop common | **Abersoch** – 'Cheshire on Sea' surfer's village | **'Tin Man' sculpture** – abstract artwork on headland above Llanbedrog

▲ *Distant Bardsey seen from the heathland on Mynydd Cilan*

Porth Neigwl/Hell's Mouth

Porth Neigwl — or 'Hell's Mouth', as it's better known — is a huge, unbroken, south-west facing four-mile long sand and shingle beach between Rhiw and Abersoch on the south coast of Llŷn. Bracketed by rocky headlands at either end, the soft boulder-clay in between is constantly being eroded by the sea. Each year, winter storms tear off another metre or so of land; and farms and houses are steadily being lost to the sea.

Because the beach faces squarely into the prevailing winds, it bears the brunt of long Atlantic swells pushing up from Cornwall and southern Ireland. In the past, this 'lee shore' was lethal to sailing ships and more than thirty are known to have been wrecked here within the last hundred years. Today, those same Atlantic swells attract surfers from all over the UK. It's one of the best and most consistent surf beaches in North Wales — a fact celebrated by Abersoch's Wakestock Surf Festival each July, when hundreds of wakeboarders throng the beach to compete in the National Championships.

'Hell's Mouth' beach in high summer

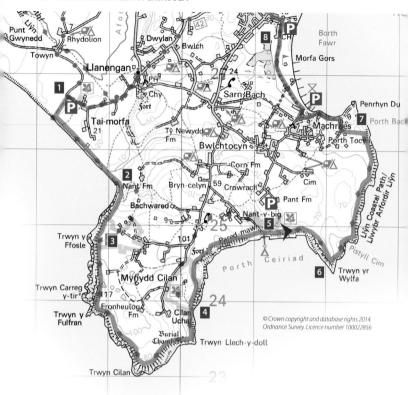

© Crown copyright and database rights 2014.
Ordnance Survey. Licence number 100022856

The route: **Hell's Mouth to Llanbedrog**

1 From the car park at **Pentowyn**, take the path down towards the beach. Turn left along the top of the dunes, above the beach, on the sandy path and continue to the far eastern end of the bay.

2 Cross the stile above the end of the beach and walk ahead up the field edge to two kissing gates. Go through the right-hand gate and walk up beside the fence on the left. Cross a wooden footbridge and continue high above the bay with increasingly spectacular views. The path runs below a line of lows cliffs to a kissing gate tight below the rocks. Go through the gate and out onto the open heath of **Mynydd Cilan**. The path rises gently through the heather and is indicated by waymarker posts.

3 At a path T-junction, turn right onto a broad grassy path which heads off across the common. Soon, the path passes beside small fields on the left to reach an **Ordnance Survey triangulation pillar** with a covered reservoir on the left.

Rare common: *Purple heather and yellow western gorse colour the common land on Mynydd Cilan*

Continue on the path beyond the triangulation pillar as it curves left around the headland. Stay on the open grass footpath following the Wales Coast Path waymarkers until directed to the left, almost at the southern tip of **Trwyn Cilan** headland.

The path now makes its way between gorse bushes and bracken to fields enclosed by walls and fences. Don't go through the gate ahead; instead, turn right and walk down beside the wall and close to the cliff edge on the right. Lower down, the path joins a section of permissive footpath enclosed by fences. Follow this to cross a **footbridge** over a stream which plunges over the cliffs as a small waterfall.

4 Beyond the footbridge, continue up steps and through a waymarked kissing gate. The path climbs steeply up the grassy, gorse-clad cliffs. For the next kilometre or so, it undulates along the cliff top passing through several kissing gates before curving slightly inland above small fields backed by high wooded cliffs.

Around 300 metres later, beyond another kissing gate, the path turns sharp right and zig-zags around a small field before heading along the top of sheer cliffs high above the western end of **Porth Ceiriad**. When the enclosed path passes through another kissing gate at the highest point, a broad panorama opens out with Abersoch, Porthmadog and the Welsh coast backed by the

Island landscape: *Looking out towards St Tudwal's Islands from Penrhyn Du*

pale line of Snowdonia's distant peaks. Notice the remains of a World War Two **observation post** immediately to the left of the path here. *The cliffs are alive with noisy jackdaws, choughs and ravens.*

From the summit, the enclosed path runs gently downhill close to the cliff edge, down steps and through yet more kissing gates before bending left and then right around a private parking area immediately above Porth Ceiriad's sandy shore. Go through the wooden kissing gate here and head across open pasture parallel to the shore. There's an emergency 'phone next to a prominent Wales Coast Path fingerpost, immediately above the beach access path.

The bay at Porth Ceiriad has a fearsome reputation and although safe bathing can be enjoyed in calm weather, great care is needed at times. However, the beach is steep and, like nearby Hell's Mouth, offers some of the best surfing in North Wales.

In 1855 the ship 'Franchise' ran aground here after losing her position in thick fog en-route to Liverpool. By the time the crew heard the breakers it was too late to turn the ship around. The crew survived but the ship was smashed to matchwood in the surf.

5 From the beach access point go ahead through the kissing gate and follow the path up through a large sloping field which rises above the beach. At the top of the rise, go through a kissing gate. The path is now straightforward and stays outside the fields on the left high above the bay.

Soon wide views open out across Cardigan Bay beyond the paired St. Tudwal's Islands, to the distant mountains of Snowdonia. Snowdon itself can be seen clearly

Lowland heath

In summer, Mynydd Cilan's heathland is bright with purple heather, yellow-flowered western gorse and emerald bilberry. A beautiful blend of coastal and maritime heath and 'unimproved' pasture, dotted with small pools, and flanked by traditional field banks—or clawdd, *this rare habitat supports lizards, adders, stonechats, wheatears and breeding choughs. It's also a great place for seawatching: with common and bottle-nosed dolphins frequently spotted just offshore.*

as the highest summit in the northern group to the left. The hills fall away, gentler and lower to the south with Cadair Idris being the highest summit.

6 Beyond **Trwyn yr Wylfa** the path turns northeast, soon crossing a wooden footbridge near **Pistyll Cim**.

When the tide is right, dolphins sometimes frolic and somersault in the cross currents off the angular headland here.

7 As the headland at Llanbedrog comes into view, the path bears left through an area of open gorse to a small foot gate. Go through the gate and along a section of enclosed footpath to reach a rough unsurfaced track.

The ruins you can see on the right of the path here are the remains of an engine house built in the 18th century to house a steam engine. The engine was used to pump water from the nearby Penrhyn Du lead mine, which operated until the 1890s and employed a large local workforce. It is similar to the buildings found at Cornish mines and may well have been built by Cornish miners who came to Llŷn because mining skills were in short supply locally. The nearby cottages called 'Cornish Row' also hint at a Cornish link.

The proximity of the sea would have been a mixed blessing here. It helped mine owners to bring heavy machinery to the area, when overland transport was poorly developed, and the lead could be loaded onto ships and transported away with ease, but flooding was a constant problem. These engine houses were essential to the success of the mines.

There are known to have been several lead mines in this area, but Penrhyn Du is thought to have been the oldest established as early as c.1638.

Turn right and follow the track down to the bay at **Machroes**. The track curves left and continues to a T-junction. Turn right here and walk down to the beach. There is boat launching access here and a car park.

The St Tudwal's Islands seen from Trwyn yr Wylfa

Welsh Riviera?: *The pretty natural harbour at Abersoch where the Afon Sôch runs into the sea*

Don't go down onto the sand unless you want to walk along the beach to Abersoch; instead, turn left along a gravel road which passes houses before heading off across the golf course.

8 At the far end of the golf course the gravel track becomes a tarmac lane with houses on the left. A little farther on, follow the lane as it swings left up the slope into town. Turn right at the T-junction and walk into 👁 **Abersoch**.

Sometimes waspishly referred to as 'Cheshire on Sea', Abersoch is probably the best known resort on the Llŷn Peninsula. With its yachts, trendy shops and restaurants, it's also been dubbed the 'Welsh Riviera'. Abersoch was once a thriving fishing village, but its natural harbour and sheltered bay made it perfect for water sports enthusiasts and today it's a curious English enclave in the heart of this otherwise Welsh cultural stronghold.

The village centre offers a variety of upmarket shops, bars, cafés and restaurants, as well as several dedicated surf shops and a boat chandlers. On summer evenings, the busy streets and lively crowds create a cosmopolitan atmosphere.

Abersoch also attracts surfing fans who head either for nearby Hell's Mouth or for 'Whistling Sands' on the other side of the peninsula, depending on the wind. The town is also popular for its annual festivals, including the RNLI New Year's

Expensive sand: *The beach chalets and static caravans on Abersoch's upmarket 'Warren' are an estate agent's dream*

Day Dip, the Wakestock wakeboarding and music festival in July, September's Abersoch Jazz Festival and the Abersoch Regatta in October.

> **Alternative route**: *Around Abersoch headland (Penbennar)*
> Turn right along 'Lôn Traeth'. This leads between large gardens before swinging left past one of Abersoch's beach car parks. Continue to the end of the road and turn left along a track. This soon becomes a footpath between gardens to reach a road end. Follow the road ahead ('Lôn Pen Cei') round into Abersoch.

9 From the centre of Abersoch, follow the main coastal road around the harbour and up the hill out of the village, towards Pwllheli. Just before '**Fach Farm' caravan site** on the left, turn right, down through the dunes of '**Trwyn y Fach**', to the beach. Turn left along the sand.

10 At the end of the beach and immediately after the final chalet, turn left up a sandy track to join a tarmac road by a car park. Turn left along the road and follow it as it rises gently, with widening views back towards Abersoch.

In just under ½ mile/1 kilometre and opposite the gate to '**Garreg-fawr**', take the signposted Wales Coast Path on the right. This leads up onto the

open headland of **Mynydd Tir-y-cwmwd**. The path climbs steeply, aided by stone steps here and there, onto the open common.

Turn right and follow the path through the bracken to a T-junction. Turn right here and follow the path around the headland, ignoring occasional minor paths to either side.

Near the front of the headland the path drops slightly near old quarry workings. *These granite quarries were worked during the early nineteenth century.*

The Tin Man

High on the headland of Mynydd Tir-cwmwd, above Llanbedrog, is Llŷn's famous 👁 '**Tin Man**'. *The first sculpture on the headland was a wooden ship's figurehead erected in 1919 by the owner of nearby Plas Glyn-y-Weddw, in Llanbedrog. It was later replaced by an iron figure of a Celtic warrior by local sculptor, Simon van de Put. When that finally rusted away, the current, more abstract 'Tin Man' was helicoptered into place, in June 2002.*

Stone was transported by ship to Liverpool and Manchester as well as France for use as road setts. Ships were sailed as far as possible up Llanbedrog beach at high tide. They were then loaded and refloated on the incoming tide. In 1900, the quarries employed some 300 local men, but work ceased abruptly with the onset of the First World War.

Ignore a junction of three paths on the left; instead, walk ahead, bearing slightly to the right, on the main Path.

As the path swings east, a fine panorama comes into view taking in the whole of Snowdonia along with the coastline east to Pwllheli and Porthmadog.

Continue to the 👁 '**Tin Man**' statue, perched on a rock platform on the edge of the cliffs overlooking the beach at Llanbedrog.

From here there is a grand view of Llanbedrog and the bay stretching east towards Pwllheli, backed by the higher summits of Snowdonia. In clear conditions you may be able to trace the line of Cardigan Bay all the way down to Pembrokeshire.

Sea view: *Llanbedrog's popular sandy beach viewed from the top of Mynydd Tir-y-cwmwd*

Snowdon can be seen as the highest summit in Snowdonia from here with the lower hills of the Moelwynion to the right, followed by the serrated skyline of the Rhinogydd and finally the high escarpment of Cadair Idris.

11 Beyond the statue, the path continues to a junction above a steep section where steps drop to the beach. Don't descend the steps; instead, take the path on the left signed to 'Plas Glyn-y-weddw'. The path contours through the woods with occasional glimpses down through the trees to the beach below. At a second junction, bear right down stone steps onto a path that descends diagonally through the woods. Pass the front of house and head down the driveway to the road in **Llanbedrog** where this Day Section ends.

Oriel Plas Glyn-y-weddw *is Wales' oldest public art gallery, established by a successful Cardiff businessman, Solomon Andrews, in 1896. Today, the Grade II Victorian Gothic mansion is home to art exhibitions, open-air theatre, outdoor sculpture, a shop and popular café.*

Detour: *A short walk to St Pedrog's Church, Llanbedrog.*
Just up the lane from the beach. *St Pedrog's church at Llanbedrog was founded in the 13th century and was on the medieval southern Pilgrims' route to Bardsey. The church was later ransacked by Cromwell's troops and much of the present building is a Victorian restoration.*

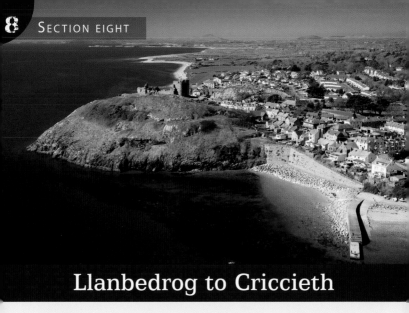

Llanbedrog to Criccieth

Distance: *15½ miles/ 25 kilometres* | **Start:** *St Pedrog's Church, Llanbedrog SH 330 316*
Finish: *Criccieth Castle SH 501 379* | **Maps:** *OS Landranger 123 Llŷn Peninsula; and OS Explorer 253 + 254 Llŷn Peninsula West and East*

Outline: An easy walk along a low, sand and shingle shore, with wide views, via the market town of Pwllheli to Criccieth and its seaside castle.

From pretty Llanbedrog, the path skirts the shore to the grassy viewpoint at Carreg y Defaid, before running above the shore and through golf links above the beach to busy Pwllheli. Beyond a nature reserve, the harbour and marina, the path follows the main A497 for a while to tiny Llanystumdwy, with its links to Lloyd George. From there, the path returns to the shore beside Afon Dwyfor then along the open coast to Criccieth with its pastel-hued guesthouses, esplanade and atmospheric medieval castle.

Services: *As the largest town on Llŷn, Pwllheli has lots of accommodation, super-markets, shops, banks, post office, pharmacy, pubs, restaurants, cafés and takeaways. Traditional open air market on Wednesdays and Sundays. Llanystumdwy has a hotel, pub and riverside café. Criccieth has accommodation, shops, banks, post office, pubs, cafés and takeaways. Pwllheli TIC 01758 613000 | pwllheli.tic@gwynedd.gov.uk*

👁 Don't miss: Llanbedrog beach huts – much photographed, multi-col-oured beach huts | **Lloyd George Museum** – Welsh Prime Minister's birthplace at Llanystumdwy | **Criccieth Castle** – superb medieval fortress on a seaside rock

▲ *Criccieth Castle high on its strategic, sea-edged rock*

Llanbedrog

Llanbedrog is a small village between Abersoch and Pwllheli on the south coast of Llŷn. The southern half of the village, below the A499, is noted for its pretty church, family pub, Plas Glyn-y-weddw art gallery, shop and café, and the sheltered sandy bay with its colourful beach huts protected by the National Trust. Overlooking the bay is the heather-clad headland of Mynydd Tir-y-cwmwd topped by its famous 'Tin Man' sculpture — with panoramic views from the summit.

Llanbedrog is named after the medieval pilgrims' church of St Pedrog. But it wasn't until the building of the Gothic dower house at Plas Glyn-y-weddw in 1856 that the village really took off. A tramway that ran along the coast from Pwllheli brought holidaymakers to the bay and at one time Llanbedrog's amenities included several hotels, a police station, sauna and dance room. Today, the combination of a sandy bay, safe bathing, beach café, beach huts and nearby toilets make it a popular place for family holidays.

Painters on the beach at Llanbedrog

Seaside homes?: *Llanbedrog's colourful beach huts in all their painted summer glory*

The route: **Llanbedrog to Criccieth**

From the end of the driveway to **Plas Glyn-y-weddw**, head down '**Lôn Nant Iago**', a short lane leading to the beach.

1 Turn left along the sandy shore passing the brightly coloured 👁 **Llanbedrog beach huts** on the left. *These are some of the most photographed beach huts in Wales. But don't expect to see them out of season; once the summer ends, the National Trust tows them to the safety of the field above, out of the reach of winter storms.*

About 150 metres beyond the final hut, look for steps on the left, which take you up onto a footpath above the shore. Follow this path, enclosed at first, through fields to the grassy headland at **Carreg y Defaid**.

The path continues beyond Carreg y Defaid passing a concrete ramp leading down onto the shore from a lane on the left. Walk on above the shore, then along the top of the sea defences to a gate. Go through the gate and follow a sandy track parallel to the embankment. This passes a bungalow and an isolated house before running beside the golf course for the next 1¼ miles/ 2 kilometres or so.

2 On the outskirts of **Pwllheli** the track swings to the left. Turn right here and follow a footpath that runs beside gardens to eventually join a road

('**Rhodfa Marian y Mor**'). Go ahead along the road again and continue ahead at a small roundabout along the promenade ('**Y Prom'**).

At the end of the promenade the road turns left and becomes '**Embankment Road**'. Turn left here with the road and follow it into the centre of Pwllheli.

*Just before the town you will see '**Lôn Cob Bach**' local nature reserve on your left. A mixture of wet pasture, reed beds and intertidal salt marsh grazed by ponies, this unusual town centre reserve is nonetheless home to ducks, swans, herons, kingfishers and otters. It is this tidal pool that gave Pwllheli its name — **pwll** (pool) **heli** (salty) — the 'salty pool'.*

At the end of Embankment Road, beyond the bridge, there is a roundabout where a left turn takes you into the centre of **Pwllheli**.

Pwllheli is Llŷn's unofficial capital and a social and political centre with a busy harbour, marina and railway station. Yet the town was granted its market charter more than 600 years ago, and as recently as the last century the town was still one of the main fishing and shipbuilding centres in North Wales. When the railway reached Pwllheli in the 1860s, the town gradually evolved

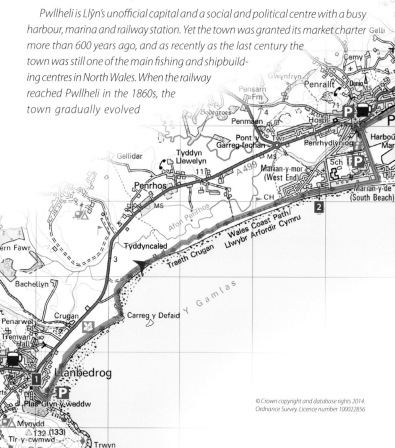

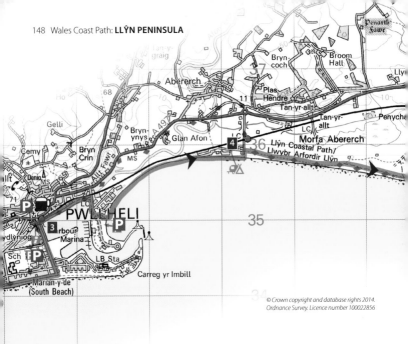

© Crown copyright and database rights 2014.
Ordnance Survey. Licence number 100022856

into the Victorian seaside resort we see today. Pwllheli's popular, traditional open-air market is held in the Square on Wednesdays and Sundays (in summer).

3 If you are not visiting **Pwllheli** turn right immediately after the bridge and before the **railway station** and roundabout and follow the road beside the **harbour**. At the end of the harbour turn right. Before you reach the **Sailing Club** bear left at a mini roundabout through the car park of the recently built 'Plas Heli' and walk down onto the beach.

4 Turn left along the beach for about 1¼ miles/ 2 kilometres.

From **Abererch Sands Caravan Park**, there is a sandy path behind the dunes which provides easier walking than continuing along the beach.

5 At the end of the beach a kissing gate in the fence ahead leads onto the pleasant grassy headland of **Pen-ychain**. Bear right around the headland to an **Ordnance Survey triangulation pillar**.

There are wide views here back along the beach to Pwllheli and ahead towards Criccieth and Moel-y-Gest, the hill that rises above Porthmadog and the end of this section of the Wales Coast Path. In clear weather you should be able to see all the way along Cardigan Bay, too.

Continue around the headland, passing behind small sand and shingle coves. Immediately before the **caravan and chalet site** (Haven), the path turns right, keeping to the outside edge of the site. At a fork, keep right again on a good path with the holiday village on the left.

6 Pass a water treatment works, cross a footbridge and go through a kissing gate into a field. The path keeps to the field edge with the rocky beach to the right. At the end of the field a kissing gate and steps lead down to the mouth of a small river — **Afon Wen**. Turn left up a rough track to reach a tarmac lane beyond a railway bridge. Follow the lane up to the main road.

The next section follows the cycleway beside the road for 2 miles/ 3.5 kilometres to the village of **Llanystumdwy**.

On the headland of Pen-ychain

River's mouth: *There's a real sense of space where the tiny Afon Dwyfor opens into the sea*

7 As the A497 approaches **Llanystumdwy**, it crosses the **Afon Dwyfor.** Less than 100 metres later, look for a Wales Coast Path signpost that points across the road to the right, to a metal gate and farm drive.

> **Detour**: *To visit the pretty little village of Llanystumdwy*
> Turn left here on a short, signposted footpath. The path runs between cottages to emerge at a junction close to the stone bridge over **Afon Dwyfor** in the heart of the village. A sign ahead points up the lane beside the river to Lloyd George's grave. **Llanystumdwy** is the birth-place of the famous British Labour Prime Minister, Lloyd George; to visit the fascinating 👁 **Lloyd George Museum**, turn right up the main street for 100 metres.

Otherwise, to continue on the **official route**, cross the main A497 and head down the horse-chestnut shaded drive, past farm buildings, to **Aberkin Farm**. Continue past the farmhouse and bear left to cross a stone stepped stile onto a rough track across the fields. Sheep and cattle graze the fields and a sign pleads 'Farmland – Keep your dog on a lead'. The track winds across the pastures to another stile and gate leading onto the **railway** line.

The single-track railway between Pwllheli and Shrewsbury is part of the picturesque Cambrian Line. The line follows a scenic route through the Cambrian Mountains of central Wales and along the coast of Cardigan Bay. Along the way, it crosses the Mawddach Estuary on the Barmouth Bridge.

8 Cross the track and continue across open fields towards **Afon Dwyfor**, with a traditional Welsh stone and earth bank, or *clawdd*, on your left. At the river bank, turn left through a waymarked metal kissing gate and follow the river

Lloyd George Museum

The great Welsh statesman David Lloyd George was born and is buried here in the tiny village of Llanystumdwy. During his time as British Prime Minister from 1916-1922, he gave women the vote and introduced the Old Age Pension. The museum is open from Easter to October and on Bank Holiday weekends. For details call 01766 522071 or see: **www.gwynedd.gov.uk/museums**

downstream. The path crosses a side stream and runs through gorse before crossing a boggy area on a raised boardwalk. The river soon kinks sharply to the right. Beyond black-painted fishermen's sheds served by a crude stone quay, Afon Dwyfor opens into **Tremadog Bay** below **Glan-y-mor**.

9 Within 100 metres of the change from turf to shingle, bear left, up onto the clear Path that runs along the top of a low, raised bluff. Now level with the fields, the rising Path traces the edge of the slope with broad views across the river mouth and Tremadog Bay to distant Harlech Castle and the jagged outline of the Rhinog hills.

Soon, a view of Criccieth opens up ahead and the path bends to the left around a spiky reedbed below **Ynysgain Fawr Farm**. *The farm's name suggests it may once have been on a large island.* The path snakes left and then right around the end of the shingly beach. The signposted Path runs alongside the beach with Criccieth town and castle clear ahead. Ignore a farm access track off to the left, and continue above the shore. The path rises gently along low bluffs. Turn right at a T-junction of paths close to **'Cefn Castell'**, and almost immediately left, along the house's clifftop access drive. Continue straight ahead through a wooden foot gate, along the top of the cliffs towards Criccieth. The surfaced Path joins the western end of the Promenade, high above the beach.

10 Walk along the promenade on **Marine Terrace** with its pastel-hued guesthouses and excellent views of the castle high on its rock

© Crown copyright and database rights 2014. Ordnance Survey. Licence number 100022856

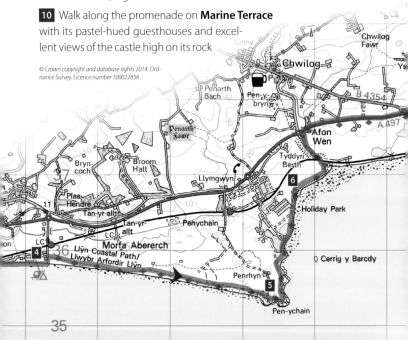

Coastal fortress: *High on its crag above the town, Criccieth Castle dominates the rocky shore ahead*

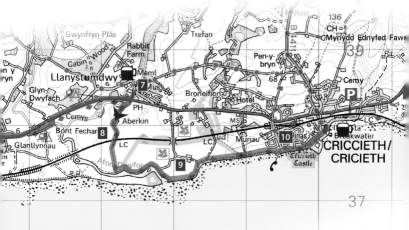

ahead. Walk uphill on the road to pass the ticket office and entrance to 👁
Criccieth Castle up to the right. Continue on the pavement over the brow
of the hill and drop down gently past cafés and antique shops back towards
the sea. Look out for Criccieth's famous ice-cream shop, **Cadwalader's**, on
the right, and then join the traditional seaside **Esplanade** above the beach
at the bottom of the slope where this Day Section ends.

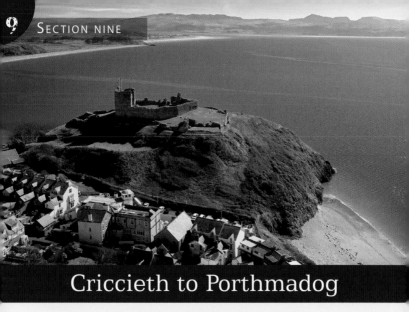

Criccieth to Porthmadog

Distance: *6½ miles/ 10.5 kilometres* | **Start:** *Criccieth Castle SH 501 379*
Finish: *Porthmadog Harbour SH 570385* | **Maps:** *OS Landranger 123 Llŷn Peninsula + 124 Dolgellau; and OS Explorer 254 Llŷn Peninsula East*

Outline: A lovely sandy section skirting the western fringe of the broad Glaslyn Estuary past Black Rock Sands and Borth-y-gest to Porthmadog.

From Criccieth town and castle, the path runs along the Esplanade before briefly following the railway line to the cliffs and caves at the western end of Black Rocks Sands. Beyond the dunes, the path crosses open sand to the rocky point at Ynys Cyngar, before curving inland along the margins of the vast and striking Glaslyn Estuary. With broad views across the tidal sands of Traeth Bach to Morfa Harlech and beyond, the route runs past picturesque Borth-y-gest and Garth to the busy harbour town of Porthmadog.

Services: *Criccieth: plenty of accommodation from hotels and B&Bs to caravan and camp sites. Good range of shops, a bank, post office, pubs, restaurants, cafés and take-aways, plus Cadwalader's famous ice cream parlour. Toilets in main car park. Camp and caravan sites around Morfa Bychan. Even more facilities in Porthmadog. Porthmadog TIC 01766 512981 | porthmadog.tic@gwynedd.gov.uk. Dukes Taxis 01766 514799*

Don't miss: Black Rock Sands – popular, long sandy beach | **Borth-y-gest** – pretty harbour village on Glaslyn Estuary | **Porthmadog Harbour** – large harbour, marina and yacht club

▲ *Criccieth Castle high on its strategic, sea-edged rock*

Criccieth

Criccieth is a charming seaside town centred on the imposing ruins of medieval Criccieth Castle. With its colourful Victorian hotels and guesthouses, traditional esplanade, sandy beaches, teashops, restaurants, pubs and ice-cream parlour, the town is a popular family holiday resort. Its position at the edge of the Snowdonia National Park also makes it a natural gateway to the Llŷn Peninsula.

Criccieth started out as little more than a church and a few houses huddled around the new castle, built as a compact Welsh fortress by Llywelyn Fawr in 1230. Yet, because of its strategic location, the castle changed hands many times and was later strengthened to become one of Edward I's 'Iron Ring' of castles. No tour of the Llŷn is complete without a visit to this fascinating castle; the view from the summit alone repays the price of a ticket.

Criccieth is also noted for its two annual fairs — held on 23rd May and 29th June — when huge crowds throng the market and fairground that fill the streets, main car park and Y Maes, or historic town common. Unmissable!

Sunrise over the Glaslyn Estuary at Borth-y-gest

Sea view: *Once home to both Welsh and English warlords, Criccieth Castle guards Tremadog Bay*

The route: **Criccieth to Porthmadog**

1 At the far end of the **Esplanade** stay with the road as it swings left. Immediately before the level crossing, take the signed coast path on the right. This runs parallel to the railway to emerge onto the stony beach. Walk ahead for 100 metres or so and turn left through a gate to cross the railway. Don't go into the field on the far side of the rails, instead turn right immediately onto a footpath that runs parallel with it again. The path emerges onto the railway briefly at one point to avoid rocks on the left, then continues beside the tracks with marshy ground over to the left.

2 Just before a river — **Afon Cedron** — cross the track again by two stiles, then head half-left across a field to join a farm track. Follow the track to the left, up the rise past a cottage, '**Ceffyl Mor**', then bear right along the access drive. Pass the '**Taliesin Lodge Park**' entrance, where you get a grand view out along the 1¾ miles/ 3 kilometre or so long beach of Black Rock Sands.

Follow the lane ahead, high above the beach and caravan sites with views beyond to the hills of the Rhiongydd and Cadair Idris.

3 Continue to a T-junction with a tarmac lane, then turn sharp right, down towards the beach. Where the road turns left, take the signed path ahead through the dunes and walk down onto **Black Rock Sands** beach.

Black Rock Sands is one of the largest stretches of sand in North Wales and is a popular and well known holiday venue. It's not the place for peace and quiet though. A boat and jet ski launching area and official car access and parking

Criccieth Castle

High on its rock, Criccieth Castle dominates this seaside town. Criccieth is the only one of Edward I's Welsh coastal fortresses built around an earlier native foundation. Much of the inner castle was built by Llywelyn ap Iowerth, or 'Llywelyn the Great', around 1230. He cruelly imprisoned his illegitimate son, Gruffydd, deep in its dungeons to prevent him becoming his successor. Criccieth's name is thought to come from two Welsh words: crug *and* caeth, *which translate literally as 'prisoner's rock'.*

*on the beach means it soon gets
crowded and is busy even in winter. Cars
overwhelmed by the incoming tide often have
to be rescued by tractors.*

Turn left along the beach and walk along the sand
for around 2 miles/3.5 kilometres.

4 At the far end of the beach there is a low grassy and rocky
headland — **Ynys Cyngar**. *This was once a tidal island but has become
part of the mainland by the build-up of dunes.*

Scramble over the low rocks to join the path around the headland. Follow
this into the small cove known as **Morfa Bychan**, the 'small shore' or 'beach'.
The path runs along the top of the sandy cove, crossing the beach access
path/track and continuing on the footpath opposite. This zig-zags up the
scrubby slopes behind the bay. At a fork, bear right as signed, and continue
up steps to reach the cliff top path.

Follow the path to an access drive, then turn right and immediately left.
Ignore a footpath on the right a little farther on, keeping ahead beside gardens on the left to reach a lane end beside an old stone cottage.

Walk ahead along the lane for 250 metres to the signed coast path on the
right. This is signed for '**Pen y Banc**' and heads down steps. At a T-junction,
turn left and follow the beach Path behind a series of coves to reach the
pretty village of **Borth-y-gest**.

5 Follow the road round onto the seafront.

*The quiet Victorian resort of Borth-y-gest overlooks the broad mouth of Afon
Glaslyn. Small boats are moored in its sheltered bay and the views from the sea-*

front are striking. The panorama looks out over the vast expanse of Traeth Mawr to the Italianate village of Portmeirion, Harlech Castle and the distant Rhinog hills.

At the far end of the seafront, the signposted Wales Coast Path bears right off the road to follow a footpath up steps. At the top, it joins an access road leading up to large houses and bungalows on the headland above. Follow

Ynys Cyngar at the mouth of the Glaslyn Estuary

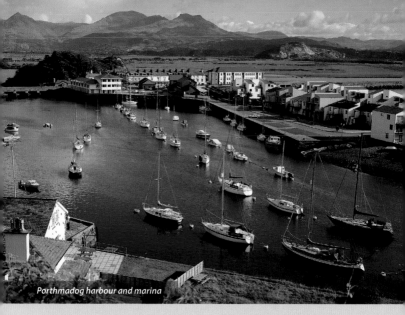

Porthmadog harbour and marina

The town that Madocks built

Porthmadog and its harbour

Before 1811, neither Porthmadog nor the dry land it stands on existed. Porthmadog and its harbour are both man-made and grew up on land reclaimed from the sea by a visionary Welshman called William Madocks. Without a moment's hesitation, Madocks named the town after himself.

William Madocks was a Georgian entrepreneur and MP who lived in London. But he also came from the Welsh landed gentry and dreamt of bringing prosperity to Wales. So, when he inherited land around Traeth Mawr, near here, he set about building an embankment, or 'cob', across the tidal estuary. This direct road and, later, rail link was part of his grand plan to create a new ferry port to Ireland at Porthdinllaen, on Llŷn. When Holyhead triumphed instead, Madocks pushed on. He completed the 'Cob', built a new harbour at Ynys y Tywyn, renamed it Port Madoc, and oversaw the birth of a new town. By 1861, Port Madoc was home to 3,000 people, most of whom worked either in the local slate quarries or shipping Welsh slates around the world.

Port Madoc prospered until the slate trade collapsed at the outbreak of the First World War. The town adopted the Welsh name Porthmadog in 1974 and today survives as a regional shopping town and popular tourist destination.

More information: For details see www.heneb

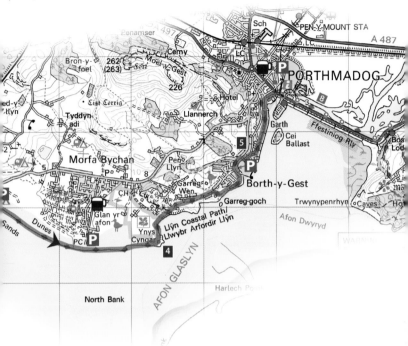

the road for 75 metres or so and where it swings left, bear right on the signed Wales Coast Path. This descends between large gardens to reach an access road on the edge of **Porthmadog Harbour**.

Porthmadog has a picturesue slate-walled harbour, popular marina and long-established yacht club. Until the beginning of the First World War, the harbour exported millions of roofing slates around the world. The returning empty ships arrived laden with ballast which they dumped in the harbour in such quantities that it formed an artificial island. It's still visible today and known as Ballast Island. The island contains rocks from all over the world, and is home to rare plants and flowers that arrived with the stones.

Follow the road ahead around the harbour's edge, past yachts and pow-erboats, to reach the **centre of Porthmadog** where the Llŷn section of the Wales Coast Path ends.

Welsh coastal place names

Welsh place names are as much a part of Wales's cultural distinctiveness as its mountains, sheep or rugged coast. To the English visitor, they may appear strangely foreign, confusing or simply unpronounceable. And yet, once carefully unravelled, they can tell us all sorts of fascinating things about a place — its landscape, character and history. Even these few common place name elements should help bring the Wales Coast Path alive.

Aber	river mouth, estuary	*Ab-er*
Afon	river	*Av-on*
Bad	ferry, boat	*Bad*
Bae	bay	*Bai*
Cae	field, enclosure	*Kai*
Carreg	stone, rock	*Kar-reg*
Cawl	sea kale	*Kowl*
Cei	quay	*Kay*
Cilfach	cove, creek	*Kil-vakh*
Clegyr	rock, cliff	*Kleg-ir*
Culfor	strait	*Kil-vor*
Din/dinas	citadel; hillfort; fortified hill	*Deen/Deen-as*
Dwr/dwfr	water	*Doer/Doo-vr*
Dyffryn	valley; bottom	*Duff-ryn*
Eglwys	church	*Eg-looees*

On Mynydd Cilan near Porth Ceiriad

Ffynnon	well; spring; fountain; source	*Fun-on*
Goleudy	lighthouse	*Gol-ay-dee*
Glan	shore	*Glan*
Gwymon	seaweed	*Gwi-mon*
Harbwr	harbour	*Haboor*
Heli	salt water, brine	*Hel-lee*
Llech	flat stone, flagstone, slate	*Th-lekh*
Maen	stone; standing stone	*Mine*
Mor	sea, ocean	*More*
Morfa	sea marsh, salt marsh	*Mor-va*
Moryd	estuary, channel	*Mor-rid*
Ogof	cave	*Og-ov*
Parrog	flat land by the sea	*Par-rog*
Penrhyn	headland	*Pen-rin*
Pigyn	point	*Pig-in*
Pont/bont	bridge, arch	*Pont/Bont*
Porth	harbour	*Porth*
Pwll	pool, pit	*Pooth*
Tafol	dock	*Tav-ol*
Ton/don	wave	*Ton/Don*
Traeth	beach	*Treye-th*
Trwyn	nose; point, cape	*Troo-een*
Tywyn	sandy shore sand dunes	*Tow-in*
Ynys	island	*Un-iss*

"Wales, where the past still lives. Where every place has its tradition, every name its poetry ..."

Matthew Arnold, *On the Study of Celtic Literature*, 1866

Visitor Information

Wales Coast Path
Comprehensive information about all sections of the Wales Coast Path can be found on the official website at **www.walescoastpath.gov.uk** and **www.walescoastpath.co.uk**

'Visit Wales'
The Visit Wales website covers everything from accommodation to attractions. For information on the area covered by this book, see: **www.visitwales. com/explore/north-wales/snowdonia-mountains-coast/explore-llyn-peninsula**

Llŷn Peninsula
For local information, from what to do to eating out, see **www.llyn.info.** Or **www.visitsnowdonia.info.** To learn more about the Llŷn's Area of Outstanding Natural Beauty, see **www.ahne-llyn-aonb.org.**

Tourist Information Centres
The Llŷn's main TICs provide free information on everything from accommodation and travel to what's on and walking advice.

Caernarfon	01286 672232	caernarfon.tic@gwynedd.gov.uk
Abersoch	01758 712929	enquiries@abersochandllyn.co.uk
Pwllheli	01758 613000	pwllheli.tic@gwynedd.gov.uk
Porthmadog	01766 512 981	porthmadog.tic@gwynedd.gov.uk

Aberdaron Visitor 'Hub'
The National Trust's new visitor centre in Aberdaron interprets the area's rich natural, historic and cultural heritage. Displays, visitor information, events and small local shops. Large 24-hour pay and display car park, beach access, safe boat launching, beach huts and toilets.

Where to stay
There's lots of accommodation close to the Wales Coast Path on Llŷn, from campsites and B&Bs to holiday cottages and hotels. Tourist Information Centre staff will know what's available locally and can even book for you. Alternatively, book online. Find camp sites at **www.ukcampsite.co.uk**

Luggage Carrying Service
Cheap, door-to-door luggage transfer between overnight stops. 'Luggage Transfer' 01437 723 030 | **www.luggagetransfers.co.uk**

Walking holidays

Several companies offer complete walking packages including: accommodation, local information, maps, baggage transfer and transport.

Celtic Trails 01291 689774 | **www.celtic-trails.com** | info@celtic-trails.com

Edge of Wales Walk 01758 760652 | **www.edgeofwaleswalk.co.uk** | enquiries@edgeofwaleswalk.co.uk

Llŷn Walking Holidays 07812 129532 | **www.llynwalkingholidays.co.uk** | enquiries@llynwalkingholidays.co.uk

Train and buses

For public transport information across Wales, see Traveline Cymru. 0871 200 22 33 | **www.traveline-cymru.info**

Cambrian Coast Line trains stop at Porthmadog, Criccieth, Penychain, Abererch and Pwllheli; from northern England, catch the train to Bangor and then the bus to Caernarfon where you can change for either Porthmadog or Pwllheli. For train times and tickets, see the Cambrian Line **www.thecambrianline.co.uk**, Arriva Trains Wales **www.arrivatrainswales.co.uk** or National Rail Enquiries **www.nationalrail.co.uk.** There are regular bus services across the peninsula, mostly radiating from Pwllheli; for downloadable timetables, search **www.gwynedd.gov.uk**

Taxis

Bangor Chubbs Cabs 01248 353535 **Caernarfon** M&R Taxis. 01286 831867 | 07785 521571| **www.caernarfontaxis.co.uk** | info@caernarfontaxis.co.uk. **Nefyn** Nefyn Taxi Service. 01758 720131. **Abersoch** Wave Cars. 07990 630 748 | **www.wavecars.co.uk** | paul@wavecars.co.uk. **Pwllheli** Stanways Taxis 07788 788044 | **www.stanwaystaxis.co.uk** | info@stanwaystaxis.co.uk. **Porthmadog** Dukes Taxis 01766 514799 |

Cycle hire

Beics Menai. Family and group cycle hire. 1 Cei Llechi, Caernarfon. 01286 676804 | 07770 951007 | **www.beicsmenai.co.uk** | hire@beicsmenai.co.uk

Llŷn Cycle Hire. Aberdaron-based family cycle hire. 01758 760 532 | 07977 586 353 | **www.llŷncyclehire.co.uk** | info@llyncyclehire.co.uk

Cycle repairs

'Bike Van'. Mobile and workshop based cycle maintenance and repair service for Gwynedd, Anglesey and Llŷn. 01286 804019 | 07805 95740

Llŷn Cycle Centre, Lower Ala Road, Pwllheli. Cycle repairs and servicing. Friendly professional advice. 01758 659043

Boat Trips

Caernarfon   Daily 40 minute pleasure cruises to the southwest entrance of the Menai Strait. 01286 672772 | 07979 593483 | **http://menaicruises.co.uk**

Aberdaron   Fast, modern boat service for Bardsey plus 3½-4½ hour day trips to the island. 07971 769895 | **www.bardseyboattrips.com**

Pwllheli   Coastal, offshore island and wildlife cruises from Pwllheli marina. 01758 612251 | **www.shearwatercruises.com**

Emergencies

In an emergency, call 999 or 112 and ask for the service your require: Ambulance, Police, Fire or Coastguard. North Wales police 01286 673347.

Tides

Short stretches of the Wales Coast Path and some alternative routes are only accessible on a low or outgoing tide. Check tide times before you go. Tide table booklets are widely available from TICs and local shops for around £1. For today's local tide information for places around Llŷn, see: **www.llyn.info/tides**

Weather forecasts

For reliable, up-to-date weather forecasts, see **www.bbc.co.uk/weather** or **www.metoffice.gov.uk/weather/uk.** For live local weather and 8 day forecasts for places around Llŷn, see **www.llyn.info/weather/**

Annual events

Llŷn Land and Seafood Festival, Pwllheli: second bank holiday in May.
Abersoch Jazz Festival: June
Criccieth Festival of music and art: June
Wakestock, Europe's largest wakeboard music festival, Abersoch: July
Abersoch Regatta: August
Llŷn Acoustic Festival, Plas Glyn-y-weddw, Llanbedrog: October
Craft Fair, Plas Glyn-y-weddw, Llanbedrog: October

Further reading

Top 10 Walks: Wales Coast Path: Llŷn Peninsula, by Carl Rogers. Northern Eye Books ISBN 978-1-908632-12-8

Walks on the Llŷn Peninsula, by Carl Rogers. Mara Books. ISBN 978-1-902512-00-6

A Llŷn Anthology, ed Dewi Roberts. Gwasg Carreg Gwalch. ISBN 978-1-84527-172-5